Editor
Lorin E. Klistoff, M.A.

Managing Editor
Karen J. Goldfluss, M.S. E.d.

Cover Artist
Tony Carrillo

Creative Director
Karen J. Goldfluss, M.S. Ed.

Art Production Manager
Kevin Barnes

Art Coordinator
Renée Christine Yates

Imaging
Leonard P. Swierski

Publisher
Mary D. Smith, M.S. Ed.

Strategies That Work!

Comprehension Practice

Grade 4

- Finding facts • Identifying main ideas
- Sequencing • Using context clues
- Drawing conclusions • Noting details
- Following directions • Using reference texts
- Understanding questions & paragraphs and more!

Includes:
- Literary & Factual Texts
- A Variety of Question Types
- Graphic Organizers

Includes Standards & Benchmarks

Author

Alan Horsfield

Teacher Created Resources, Inc.
6421 Industry Way
Westminster, CA 92683
www.teachercreated.com

ISBN: 978-1-4206-8044-7

© 2007 Teacher Created Resources, Inc.
Made in U.S.A.

Teacher Created Resources

TABLE OF CONTENTS

Strategies in This Book

This book is intended to help students develop successful strategies for reading comprehension. The students accomplish this by reading passages and articles and then answering a variety of questions using a specific strategy. When the student completes the exercises, he or she will have practiced a strategy and worked through a number of question types from a variety of texts.

Rather than give a range of strategies for each passage, the focus will be on developing the student's skill in applying one particular strategy. The book is structured so that if a student is having difficulty in one area, he or she can concentrate on a strategy that will help improve comprehension. The strategies included in this book are listed below.

STRATEGIES

Each new section provides information on what is required for the particular strategy being practiced. The first introduction page in each section is intended to lead the student through a given strategy. The answers for the questions are provided at the bottom of the introduction exercise page. The answers for the rest of the section pages are provided in the back of the book.

Text Types

In addition to providing strategy practice, this book also offers a range of text types so the student will feel confident in a variety of situations. Text types are usually broken into two broad categories. Within each group are a number of choices—some are listed below.

- *Literary texts*—include narratives (novels/stories), poetry, and scripts (drama)

- *Factual texts*—include explanations, expositions, information reports, recounts, and procedures

As one can see, the list is quite long. It is important that students develop comprehension skills from a variety of text types.

(*Note to Teacher:* In this book, on a number of occasions, the passages are reused. This is done to demonstrate that a variety of comprehension strategies can be applied to the same piece of writing. Comprehension skills are interdependent.)

Question Types

Question types included in this book are as follows:

- true/false responses
- short answers
- matching exercises
- sequencing

- multiple-choice responses
- full sentence answers
- sentence completion
- open-ended responses

Standards

The standards and benchmarks that are listed on page 5 will be met or reinforced by completing the practice pages included in this book. These standards and benchmarks are similar to the ones required by your state and school district. The standards and benchmarks are taken from *A Compendium of Standards and Benchmarks for K–12 Education* (Copyright 2004 McREL, www.mcrel.org/standards-benchmarks) Language Arts (Grades 3–5). They are displayed in a simple-to-read reference chart. The chart shows the pages to which the standard and benchmarks specifically refer.

Graphic Organizers

At the end of the book, there are a variety of graphic organizers to help your students organize their ideas and concepts when reading a certain passage and working on a certain strategy. Learners of all kinds will be able to visualize their information and ideas when familiar with graphic organizers. Students will be better able to access, understand, organize, and present information.

REFERENCE CHART

Standard: Uses the general skills and strategies of the writing process

Benchmark: Writes in response to literature — All Pages

Standard: Uses the stylistic and rhetorical aspects of writing

Benchmark: Uses a variety of sentence structures in writing — All Pages

Standard: Uses the general skills and strategies of the reading process

Benchmark: Establishes a purpose for reading — All Pages

Benchmark: Uses phonetic and structural analysis techniques, syntactic structure, and semantic context to decode unknown words — Pages 28–33

Benchmark: Uses a variety of context clues to decode unknown words — Pages 28–33

Benchmark: Uses word reference materials — Pages 58–61

Benchmark: Understands level-appropriate reading vocabulary — All Pages

Benchmark: Monitors own reading strategies and makes modifications as needed — All Pages

Benchmark: Adjusts speed of reading to suit purpose and difficulty of material — All Pages

Standard: Uses reading skills and strategies to understand and interpret a variety of literary texts

Benchmark: Uses reading skills and strategies to understand and interpret a variety of literary passages and texts — Pages 11, 15, 18, 20–23, 25–30, 32–37, 39–40, 44–45, 50, 53–56

Benchmark: Understands the basic concept of plot — Pages 11, 15, 18, 20–23, 25–27, 34–37, 39–40, 44–45, 50, 53–56

Standard: Uses reading skills and strategies to understand and interpret a variety of informational texts

Benchmark: Uses reading skills and strategies to understand a variety of informational texts — Pages 6–10, 12–14, 16–17, 19, 24, 31, 38, 41–43, 46–49, 51–52, 57, 62–63, 64–65

Benchmark: Uses the various parts of a book — Pages 62–63

Benchmark: Summarizes and paraphrases information in texts — Pages 14–21

*All standards listed above are from *A Compendium of Standards and Benchmarks for K–12 Education* (Copyright 2004 McREL, www.mcrel.org/standards-benchmarks) Language Arts (Grades 3–5).

Name: _____   Date: _____

INTRODUCTION

How should you begin to look for facts in written works? When **finding facts**, you will often be asked questions beginning with *who, when, where, what, how,* and sometimes *why*. You will be asked to search for answers to questions that help you understand the time and place of the action in the passage, as well as who or what is involved. The words in parentheses will help you find the facts. Sometimes you will be asked to give names or make lists.

Most exercises in this part of the book are based upon factual writing. The passage, *Dugong, Dive!*, is a piece of factual writing and is a good place to start finding facts. In this passage, each short paragraph gives another dugong fact.

Unless told to do otherwise, you should answer with complete sentences to help you understand the questions and think through your responses.

Now read this passage from *Dugong, Dive!* by Jill Morris

FACTS ABOUT DUGONGS

(What) The dugong is an aquatic mammal. It lives in the sea and suckles its young. Its scientific name is *dugong dugon*.

The dugong is about 3 meters long and weighs about 300 kilograms. The male is larger and heavier than the female. *(size of dugongs)*

The dugong's face is broad, with tiny eyes and a snout like a pig's. Its mouth is wide and its lips are thick and blubbery. Its nostrils are round wells which snap shut when the dugong dives. *(dugong's facial features)*

The dugong has two flippers and a tail with two triangular flukes like a whale's. Its hide is smooth, though often covered in barnacles. *(appearance)*

The adult male has two short brown tusks above its upper teeth. It uses these sharp tusks for defense. The female also has tusks, but they are so short that they cannot be seen. *(tusks)*

(Where) The dugong lives in water but breathes air, like all mammals. It has to surface to breathe every few minutes; otherwise it would drown. It can stay under the water for up to eight minutes if danger threatens. *(behavior)*

---

1. *What* is a dugong? _____

2. *Where* do dugongs live? _____

3. The second paragraph tells the reader about the _____ of dugongs.

4. The fourth paragraph has facts about the dugong's (face   flippers   tusks). (Circle one word.)

5. For what are the tusks of the male used? _____

_____

Answers:
1. A dugong is an aquatic mammal that lives in the sea. 2. Dugongs lives in water (or the sea). 3. size
4. flippers 5. The tusks (of the male) are used for defense.

Name: _____ Date: _____

HEARTY FACTS

by Shane Power

Here are some curious facts about your heart. See how many you already know!

❤ Your heart is a very strong pump. It is divided into four chambers, two on the left side, two on the right. A wall of muscle separates each side.

❤ Your heart is made of muscle and is a reddish color.

❤ It has lots of jobs to do every day, with no time off for sleep or play.

❤ An adult's heart weighs about 300 grams. That's about the same size as a small grapefruit.

❤ A normal heart beats 60–80 times per minute. Children's hearts beat faster, at about 100–120 times per minute. During exercise, heartbeats can increase to 200 beats per minute. Whew! That's a lot of work for one heart. Try counting the beats. (You may need a stopwatch.)

❤ Your heart is an amazing pump, made up of strong muscle. It is always pumping, sending blood to all parts of your body. Your heart pumps 90 milliliters of blood for every beat when you are sitting still. That's as much as two gulps of water.

1. *What* is this passage about? _____

2. *How* many times does a normal adult heart beat in a minute? _____

_____

3. *How* many times does a child's heart beat in a minute? _____

_____

4. *What* does the heart do? _____

_____

5. Write one fact you learned from the passage. _____

_____

Name: _____   Date: _____

KITES

by David Bowden & Jenny Dibley

The Birthplace of Kites

Kites have been flown in China since about 400 B.C., around the time when work began on the Great Wall of China.

Chinese kites were often used for military purposes.

One of the earliest accounts tells how a general, Han Xian, was trying to invade a heavily guarded palace. He flew a kite over the wall of the palace, then measured the length of the kite string to calculate the distance required to reach inside the palace.

Using that measurement as a guide, Han Xian tunnelled secretly under the wall of the palace and took the defenders by surprise.

During the Han Dynasty (202 B.C.–A.D. 220), kites were also used in battle, to scare the enemy. They were fitted with hummers made from bamboo pipes. These made eerie sounds as the kites flew over sleeping soldiers in their camps.

The soldiers would awake terrified at the sound of mysterious attacking monsters and flee their camp, leaving their weapons and belongings behind.

1. Where were kites first used? _____

_____

2. How were kites used in the Han Dynasty? _____

_____

Tell whether these facts are *True* or *False*.

3. Kites were used to build the Great Wall of China. _____

4. Soldiers were frightened by the noise that came from the kites. _____

5. One of the first stories about kites tells how they were used to invade a palace. _____

6. Circle the words that describe how kites were used in Ancient China.

   pleasure   military   monsters   children   measuring

GOLDEN WOMBATS

by Jill Morris

Jill Morris has called her passage a <u>report</u>. Reports provide the reader with facts.

The Mystery of the Golden Wombats

Jill Morris reports:

In 1980 I saw the carcass of a wombat which had been shot in a field on the east coast of Flinders Island. It didn't look like an ordinary wombat. It had golden fur.

Years later, I saw nine wombats with pale golden fur, feeding on a hillside in the center of the island.

Many of the wombats on Flinders Island have silver-grey fur, like other common wombats. The light-colored variation seems to be quite rare.

Why are these wombats golden?

Is it because they are old and their dark fur has gone pale with age?

No—because some I saw looked young.

Is it because their fur has been bleached by the sun?

No—because the fur is the same color all over the wombat's bodies: back, head, and legs.

Is it because the soil in that area is lacking in some mineral, and that makes the animals' fur lighter in color?

I saw golden wombats in two different areas. I don't think the color is caused by the food they eat or the soil where it grows. I think the variation in fur color is genetic—meaning that the wombats are born with it.

1. What mystery was Jill Morris trying to solve? _____

_____

2. What color is the fur of most wombats on Flinders Island? _____

_____

3. Give one reason that Jill Morris considered when trying to work out why some wombats

were a different color. _____

_____

4. Where did Jill Morris see her first golden wombat?

_____

_____

_____

5. Where else did Jill see golden wombats?

_____

Name: _____   Date: _____

BOBBY BOY

by Errol Broome

Young Tommy Woodcock helped with the horses in Mr. Telford's Sydney stables.

Tommy was small and shy and his voice was gentle. He did not look tough enough to handle the sturdy animals. But his arms were strong, and he understood horses. He talked to them, rubbed them down, and coaxed them until they did as they were told.

The horses did not win many races. But there was always hope. Perhaps, one day, one of them would win the Melbourne Cup. Anyone can hope.

One summer's day, Mr. Telford's new horse arrived. Tommy called him Bobby Boy because his real name was too grand for the poor, straggly yearling that limped off the ship from New Zealand. How could this animal ever live up to the name of Phar Lap? It meant "lightning"! One thing looked certain—he would never win the Melbourne Cup.

People laughed at the horse and called him a donkey. Tommy did not think it was funny because, from the start, he and Bobby were friends. The horse came when Tommy called and refused to eat from anyone but him. Mr. Telford saw that Tommy was good for the new horse. "All right, Tommy." he said. "Phar Lap is your job."

1. What did Tommy Woodcock do for a living? _____

_____

2. The second paragraph gives the reader information on

   (A) winning the Melbourne Cup.

   (B) Bobby Boy's appearance.

   (C) Tommy Woodcock's character.

   (D) how people reacted to the New Zealand horse.

3. Who was Mr. Telford? _____

4. What does the name "Phar Lap" mean? _____

5. How did Tommy treat the horses? _____

6. Draw a checkmark to choose the best way to complete this sentence.

   No one thought that Bobby Boy would

   [ ] eat the food given to him.

   [ ] win the Melbourne Cup.

   [ ] stop limping.

SHINER

by Marilyn Cosgrove

This passage is part of a true story.

The Smiling Bull-terrier with the Black Eye-patch

A bull terrier is not everyone's idea of a good-looking dog, but Pat and George thought their new puppy was beautiful.

They lived in a new house and they meant her to be an outside dog, but the puppy decided that their bedroom was the place to sleep. No hot water bottles or ticking clocks would comfort this puppy. She just wanted to be near George and Pat.

A few restless nights soon turned into nights of contentment.

Pat and George found it hard to choose a name for this smiling bull-terrier with the black eye-patch. Then George, a part-time wrestler, came home one night with a black eye.

"What a shiner!" cried Pat as she helped him through the door. She laughed when she noticed the puppy's puzzled expression. From that moment on, "Shiner" was the perfect name for a bull-terrier with one black eye!

It soon turned out that choosing a name for the puppy was the least of their problems. Shiner chewed everything she could sink her sharp little teeth into, and she left messes in the most undesirable of places. She took the clean laundry from the clothes line and "helped" in the garden. But if you've ever had a mischievous puppy, you'll know that George and Pat couldn't help loving Shiner. In fact, they loved her more and more each day.

Make a check in the box next to the answer that best completes the sentence.

1. At first, Pat and George wanted Shiner to

☐ be a good-looking pup.   ☐ wrestle with George.

☐ sleep in the bedroom.   ☐ be a pup that lived outdoors.

2. The pup was called Shiner because she

☐ had a bright smile.   ☐ was always up to mischief.

☐ looked as if she had a black eye.   ☐ chewed up everything she could find.

3. How did George get his black eye? _____

_____

4. Shiner got her black eye when "helping" in the garden.   True ☐

False ☐

5. Pat and George wanted an outside dog because they had a new house.   True ☐

False ☐

FINDING FACTS

Name: _____   Date: _____

NAMES ARE FUN

by Vivienne Wallington

Er . . . What's Your Name?

Have you noticed that people we don't know very well sometimes forget our names when they meet us again? Perhaps they have a bad memory for names—or perhaps they are just simply forgetful. Don't let it bother you. It doesn't mean anything except that they have a bad memory! They are not doing it on purpose.

Even the people closest to us can stumble over our names at times. Parents, for instance, have so much on their minds that sometimes they can find themselves muddling up the names of their own children!

I remember a girl called Kimberley who had a pet dog called Benjamin and a brother called Christopher. Her father was forever calling her "Ben-Chris-Kim."

I have two brothers called Stan and Howard. My mother often used to call me "Stan-How-Viv."

If something like this happens to you, don't worry about it. Your parents know perfectly well what your name is.

---

1. According to the passage, what do many people forget? _____

_____

2. What did Kimberly's father sometimes call her? _____

3. Who is Viv? _____

4. Draw a line to connect the beginning of each sentence with its correct ending.

Parents have so much to think about	they haven't done it on purpose.
Some people who forget names	they can forget their children's names.
If friends forget your name,	have bad memories.

5. Parents often _____ over names as they try to remember the right name.

6. If your parents forget your name, they haven't _____ who you are.

7. When someone forgets your name, you shouldn't let it _____ you.

8. Parents are the only people to forget the names of children.

True ☐   False ☐

Name: _____   Date: _____

A MONSTER WILL GET YOU
by Edel Wignell

Monsters of the World

People everywhere tell monster stories.

Among the settlers who came to Australia two hundred years ago were people from China, Italy, and Greece. Now, after two centuries of migration, Australia is home to people from more than 140 cultures.

Australian children today may hear the monster stories that their parents or grandparents were told in Vietnam, Lebanon, Holland, Chile, and other countries all over the world. Here are just a few.

In Laos, some parents say, "If you are naughty, Kongkoi will get you!" This monster, which lives in the forest, looks like a hairy monkey whose feet are on back to front — toes pointing backwards. He attacks adults who use bad language in the forest. He also punishes children who are rude to adults or who misbehave by swimming in streams when it is forbidden.

In China and Thailand some children fear gwee (ghosts), which live in ponds and rivers. They look like little monkeys. When children go into the water, the gwee grabs them and holds them underwater until they drown.

1. What is the Kongkoi? _____

_____

2. Where are gwee supposed to live? _____

_____

3. In Australia, there are many different monster stories because

☐ settlers have been there for two hundred years.

☐ Australian parents think their children are naughty.

☐ children misbehave and are rude to adults.

☐ people in Australia come from many different cultures.

4. The Kongkoi punishes adults, as well as children.   True ☐   False ☐

5. The Kongkoi and the gwee look like monkeys.   True ☐   False ☐

6. Stories about monsters

☐ have been passed down through the ages.

☐ are based on true events.

Name: _____ Date: _____

INTRODUCTION

You might have already read part of the following passage, in which you practiced finding facts. Now let's read *Bobby Boy* to try **finding the main idea**.

When reading paragraphs, you will often be asked to find the main idea. The main idea is often the same as the <u>topic sentence</u>. It is the most important piece of information for the reader. All other sentences in the paragraph add to the meaning of the topic sentence. They are often called <u>supporting details</u>.

The topic sentence is often the first sentence, but it can come in the middle of the paragraph or at the end. You will be asked to search for answers to questions that help you understand the story. The topic sentence, if it is quite long, may sometimes contain more information than just the main idea.

Paragraphs are usually made up of more than one sentence. (See Understanding Paragraphs, page 54.) Titles and headings often give the main idea of a book or of a chapter. If we look at the story *Bobby Boy* again, we use it to start finding the main idea. Any piece of writing can be used for more than one type of comprehension question.

Now read the passage *Bobby Boy* by Errol Broome.

> Young Tommy Woodcock helped with the horses in Mr. Telford's Sydney stables. (*main idea/topic sentence*; There is no supporting detail in this paragraph.)
>
> Tommy was small and shy and his voice was gentle. (*main idea/topic sentence*) He did not look tough enough to handle the sturdy animals. But his arms were strong, and he understood horses. He talked to them, rubbed them down, and coaxed them until they did as they were told. (*supporting detail;* The last three sentences support the main idea and give the reader more information about the shy and gentle Tommy.)
>
> The horses did not win many races. (*main idea/topic sentence*) But there was always hope. Perhaps, one day, one of them would win the Melbourne Cup. Anyone can hope. (*supporting detail*)
>
> One summer's day, Mr. Telford's new horse arrived. (*main idea/topic sentence*) Tommy called him Bobby Boy because his real name was too grand for the poor, straggly yearling that limped off the ship from New Zealand. How could this animal ever live up to the name of Phar Lap? It meant "lightning"! One thing looked certain—he would never win the Melbourne Cup. (*supporting detail*)

1. How many paragraphs are in this passage? _____

2. How many topic sentences would you expect to find? _____

3. Give two words that help describe Bobby Boy. (supporting detail in Paragraph 4)

   a. _____   **b.** _____

4. Circle the best title for this passage.

    The New Horse   The Melbourne Cup   Rubbing Down Horses

Answers:
1. four 2. four 3. a. poor b. straggly (Other possible answers: lame/limping, yearling) 4. The New Horse

QUIET PONY FOR SALE
by Mary Small

When Hannah came with her parents to live in the small country town of Bakers Flat, she had to catch the bus to school each day. On the first morning, while she was waiting at the end of the road for the bus to arrive, she saw a sign nailed to a gate on the other side of the highway. "Quiet pony for sale," it read.

Hannah loved horses. That afternoon, back from school, she went to the gate and looked over. There in the middle of the paddock was the pony. His rough coat was matted with mud, his mane and tail were long and scraggly. He stared at her with sad brown eyes.

"Here, pony!" said Hannah, stretching out her hand. She felt annoyed that she had nothing to give him.

The pony stood still.

"I'll bring you something tomorrow," said Hannah, and she hurried home.

The next morning, she took two apples for her lunchbox. Back from school, she went straight to the gate. The pony was busy grazing.

"Here, pony!" called Hannah, holding out an apple. "Come on! Look what I've got for you."

1. How many paragraphs are in this story? _____

2. What is the topic sentence of the second paragraph? _____

_____

3. What did Hannah do in paragraph 6? The next morning, Hannah _____

_____

4. Paragraph 1 tells the reader

☐ about Hannah's day at school.

☐ how Hannah came to see the notice.

☐ what the pony looked like.

☐ what Hannah fed the pony.

5. What did the pony do when Hannah called it the first time? _____

_____

6. Which of these would be another good title for this story?

☐ Apples for Lunch   ☐ A Day at School

☐ Sad Eyes   ☐ Making Friends

7. What important information can you learn from paragraph 2?

_____

Name: _____   Date: _____

BOBBY BOY
by Errol Broome

You might have already read part of the following passage, in which you practiced finding facts and finding the main idea. Now read *Bobby Boy* to try finding more main ideas.

After his big win, Phar Lap was a hero. People came from everywhere just to look at him. He had become the second highest money winner in the world.

Phar Lap was entered in the world's top races at Arlington (USA) in July. Meanwhile Tommy took him for a vacation near San Francisco. Every night, he slept outside Phar Lap's stall. At dawn each day he greeted the horse with a lump of sugar.

One morning, Phar Lap refused the sugar. Tommy could tell he was sick. He called the vet, but the horse grew steadily worse. This time, Tommy could not save his life.

In the early afternoon of April 5, 1932, Phar Lap died, while Tommy clung crying to his neck.

The news flashed to Australia: *Phar Lap is dead!* Radio programs were interrupted. People stood in the streets. The nation mourned.

1. How many paragraphs are in this passage? _____

2. Draw a line to match the paragraph number with the main idea of that paragraph.

Paragraph 1   Phar Lap comes to the USA.

Paragraph 2   Phar Lap becomes a hero.

Paragraph 3   Phar Lap dies.

Paragraph 4   Phar Lap gets sick.

3. What would be another good title for this passage?

☐ The Death of Phar Lap   ☐ The Radio News

☐ Sugar for a Winner   ☐ Winning Money

4. Which paragraph tells the reader about what Tommy did on his vacation?

☐ Paragraph 1   ☐ Paragraph 2   ☐ Paragraph 3   ☐ Paragraph 4

5. Circle the letter next to the main idea of the last paragraph.

(A) The news flashed to Australia: *Phar Lap is dead!*

(B) Radio programs were interrupted.

(C) People stood in the streets.

(D) The nation mourned.

CUNNING RUNNING
by Elizabeth Best

What Is Orienteering?

Orienteering is a sport which began in Europe in 1918. It is very popular in Scandinavia. In Sweden, an annual five-day orienteering event attracts over 15,000 participants.

To "orient" yourself means to work out where you are. In orienteering, people run or walk around a course, using a compass and a map to find their way.

Orienteering is known as the "O sport." Sometimes it is called the "thought sport," because orienteers need to think about where the controls might be and when they should run.

Another name for orienteering is "cunning running," because you must think about the best way to go. Which route should you choose? Should you run down the long track or climb over the big hill?

How Do You Do It?

Runners use a compass and map to find red and white markers in the bush. The markers are called controls.

Each runner chooses a course. There are easy, or novice, courses for beginners. There are harder courses for runners or walkers who have done orienteering before. And there are very hard, or elite, courses for the best runners.

Who Does It?

Orienteering is popular with people of all ages, in many parts of the world.

Orienteering began in Australia in 1969. In 1985, the world championships were held in this country. They were run in the outback near Bendigo, in Victoria. Orienteers came from Scandinavia, France, Hong Kong, Japan, the USA, New Zealand, and many other countries.

---

1. How many paragraphs are in this passage? _____

2. Draw a checkmark next to the main idea of the last paragraph.

- [ ] Orienteering began in Australia in 1969.
- [ ] In 1985, the world championships were held in this country.
- [ ] They were run in the outback near Bendigo, in Victoria.
- [ ] Orienteers came from many other countries.

3. What would be another good title for this passage?

- [ ] How to Enjoy Orienteering
- [ ] History of Orienteering in Australia
- [ ] Orienteering, the Latest Sport
- [ ] Let's Learn About Orienteering

4. Under which subheading would you look to find out what orienteering is?

_____

5. Orienteering is only for fit and healthy adults.   True [ ]   False [ ]

JOANNE
by Paul Williams

Joanne's father owned a general store and sandwich shop in Bondi, a Sydney beachside suburb. Joanne and her dad lived at the back of the shop in four tiny, cluttered, and usually untidy rooms. Mom had died when Joanne was three. Joanne had wonderful memories of her mother. Memories of a soft voice, cuddles, bedtime stories, and having her hair brushed.

Joanne loved her father and their home. She had always been her dad's girl, although she had her mother's smile. Dad read her stories and gave her cuddles, too, but it was difficult for him to make time for an eight year old. He opened the shop at 6 o'clock in the morning and didn't finish until 9 o'clock at night. Then there was the cooking and the housework to be done and Joanne's school clothes to be washed and ironed every night.

Just before storytime, Joanne would go into the shop and share a milkshake with her father. Dad's milkshakes were a real treat: double milk, malt, two scoops of ice cream, and chocolate flavoring.

---

1. What is the main idea of paragraph 1? _____

_____

2. What is paragraph 2 mostly about?

☐ Joanne's life with her father   ☐ Joanne's memories of her mother

☐ getting meals at the sandwich shop

3. The last paragraph is mostly about

☐ sharing.   ☐ working.   ☐ making milkshakes.   ☐ telling stories.

4. The story is mostly about

☐ Joanne's mother.   ☐ Joanne.   ☐ Joannes's father.

5. The information about opening the shop is supporting detail.   True ☐   False ☐

6. Joanne could hardly remember her mother.   True ☐   False ☐

Name: _____   Date: _____

THE TOOTH BOOK

by Viki Wright

The earliest false teeth were probably used for decorative rather than practical reasons.

For example, the ancient Egyptians believed that important people who died went on to an afterlife, so they would replace missing teeth in the mouths of dead kings to make them look nice in the next world. These teeth were lightly wired into place and could never have been used for chewing.

Later, the Phoenicians (1000 B.C.–700 B.C.) made the first sets of false teeth, held together by gold wire.

Around the same time (800 B.C.–600 B.C.), the Etruscans knew how to clamp gold bands around teeth that were still firmly attached, so that single false ones could be held in place next to them. The false teeth were carved from the teeth of oxen or other animals.

Throughout history, people have tried to make false teeth that would work properly and look good. The early dentists did the best they could and contributed a lot of knowledge to those who followed them. Dentists have always been quick to use the newest technology to improve their work.

People who fixed teeth were not called dentists in the olden days. Different people tried to do parts of the work that dentists do today. Priests who believed that a toothache was the work of the devil prayed for the person to be freed from the curse of pain. Herbalists created strange mixtures to paint on teeth or feed to the sufferer. The local barber doubled as a dentist, and the local blacksmith, who was often very strong, was used to pull out teeth.

1. How many paragraphs are in this passage? _____

2. Write the topic sentence for the last paragraph. _____

_____

3. Draw a line to show the order in which these people appear in the passage.

first   the Phoenicians

second   the Egyptians

third   the Etruscans

4. Which paragraph tells the reader how dentists keep up with new ideas? paragraph ____

5. Which of these would be another good title for this passage?

☐ Going to the Dentist   ☐ The Ancient Egyptians

☐ The History of False Teeth   ☐ The First Dentists

FINDING THE MAIN IDEA

SPOOKED!

by Errol Broome

Gerry's house was the creepiest house on the street. It had rickety stairs and odd-shaped rooms full of dark corners, and a gabled roof that looked like a witch's hat. It was exactly the sort of place where you would expect to find something peculiar.

"I'm not scared," said Hank, who lived at number 37 Oak Street. He swung open Gerry's closet door. The hinges creaked, but the inside looked like any closet. It was a mess.

"There's nothing there," said Hank. "Just clothes and shoes and stuff."

Gerry didn't like the noises himself — not one bit. That's why he kept asking friends to stay. He had tried almost every boy on Oak Street, and they only came once. Now it was Hank's turn.

"Can't we leave the light on?" asked Hank. "That way we're sure to be safe."

"I've got a flashlight," said Gerry. "But, okay, we can try the light too."

---

1. How many paragraphs are in this story? _____

2. Draw lines to identify the main idea and the supporting details of the first paragraph.

Main Idea

rickety stairs

a gabled roof that looked like a witch's hat

Supporting Details

description of Gerry's house

dark corners

3. Paragraph 4 is mostly about

☐ the creaky closet door.

☐ the number of boys who stayed at Gerry's place.

☐ the boys of Oak Street.

☐ Gerry's reason for inviting friends to sleep over.

4. Which paragraph tells you about Hank's inspection? Paragraph _____

5. Which of these would be another good title for this story?

☐ Brave Hank

☐ The Flashlight

☐ The Witch's House

☐ The Messy Closet

6. The closet was full of mysterious things.   True ☐

False ☐

Name: _____   Date: _____

MR. GREYFINCH'S GARDEN

by Bernard Lloyd and Coral Tulloch

Mr. Greyfinch was moving. He waved good-bye to his city apartment and moved everything he owned to a cottage in the suburbs.

It was a small house, but it was surrounded by a large garden. Mr. Greyfinch thought that all the people who lived in such a peaceful place must be kind and friendly.

For the first few weeks, Mr. Greyfinch busied himself unpacking and sorting his small treasures, until everything was in its proper place.

Mr. Greyfinch would often sit in the early morning sun on the veranda and watch his garden.

Someone before him, a long time ago, had planted orange, lemon, and plum trees. Choko and passionfruit vines hung across neighboring fences, and, beneath the chili bushes, there were sprawling clumps of herbs.

1. Draw a line to match the paragraph number with the main idea of that paragraph.

   Paragraph 1   the garden

   Paragraph 3   moving in

   Paragraph 5   the new home

2. Copy one of the paragraphs that has only one sentence. _____

   _____

3. Which of these would be another good title for this story?

   ☐ Going on Vacation   ☐ The Fruit Trees

   ☐ Getting Old   ☐ Moving to a New House

4. Mr. Greyfinch's house was large with a small garden.   True ☐

                                                           False ☐

5. Mr. Greyfinch went to live in the country.   True ☐

                                                 False ☐

6. For a few weeks after moving in, Mr. Greyfinch

   (planted chokos   waved good-bye to his city apartment   unpacked his belongings).

   (Circle one answer.)

Name: _____   Date: _____

INTRODUCTION

You might have already read the following story, in which you practiced finding the main idea. Now let's read *Quiet Pony for Sale* to try sequencing events.

Sequencing refers to the order in which things are done or the order in which they happen. Directions are given in a sequence which we are meant to follow. Directions are used in recipes, training programs, exams, and doing magic tricks. (See page 46.)

In most stories, we read about events that follow one after another. Sometimes authors present the sequence of events out of order to make their stories interesting and mysterious. Diaries are a good example of events happening in a time sequence.

The story, *Quiet Pony for Sale*, is a realistic story, so it is a good book to start understanding sequencing. In sequencing, you should understand such terms as *before, after, then, during, later,* and *earlier.* You should answer with complete sentences, unless told to do otherwise.

Now read the passage from *Quiet Pony for Sale* by Mary Small.

> When Hannah came with her parents to live in the small country town of Bakers Flat, she had to catch the bus to school each day. On the first morning, while she was waiting at the end of the road for the bus to arrive, she saw a sign nailed to a gate on the other side of the highway. "Quiet pony for sale," it read.
>
> Hannah loved horses. That afternoon, back from school, she went to the gate and looked over. There in the middle of the paddock was the pony. His rough coat was matted with mud, his mane and tail were long and scraggly. He stared at her with sad brown eyes.
>
> "Here, pony!" said Hannah, stretching out her hand. She felt annoyed that she had nothing to give him.
>
> The pony stood still.
>
> "I'll bring you something tomorrow," said Hannah, and she hurried home.
>
> The next morning, she took two apples for her lunchbox. Back from school, she went straight to the gate. The pony was busy grazing.

1. What did Hannah see on the first morning on her way to school?

_____

2. What did Hannah do on the second morning? _____

_____

3. On the first afternoon, when Hannah called the pony, it _____ .

4. Which event happened first?   A. Hannah and her parents went to live in the country.

B. Hannah went to school on a bus.

Answers:

1. Suggested answer: Hannah saw a sign nailed to a gate on the other side of the highway. 2. Hannah put two apples in her lunchbox. 3. stood still 4. A. Hannah and her parents went to live in the country.

Name: _____   Date: _____

CHARLIE'S FISH AND OTHER TALES
by R. L. Muddyman

Charlie couldn't wait to give it a try. So as soon as he had unloaded the cart, he headed off to a quiet bend of the river to catch a fish.

For three days, he sat there without a bite. Early on the fourth day, just as the sun was rising, Charlie woke up to the sound of waves crashing on to the riverbank. He opened his eyes and there, cruising down the middle of the river, was what looked like the sails of a Spanish galleon. Charlie knew right away what it really was—the dorsal fin of a huge Murray cod!

Quick as a flash, Charlie tied the end of his line to the horse team and took up the slack. When the big fish took the bait, the jolt was so great that it dragged the bend right out of the river.

For two days Charlie fought that fish. Neither one of them gave an inch. Then, just at sunset on the second day, Charlie felt the fish was starting to tire.

With a crack of his great whip and a mighty roar, Charlie urged his team forward. They heaved and pulled all night, and by the early hours of the morning, the mighty Murray cod lay high and dry on the riverbank. The water level dropped three meters the moment the fish cleared the river—and even Charlie was surprised.

---

1. When did Charlie head for the river bend? _____

   _____

2. Number the boxes 1 through 4 to show the order of events.

   [ ] Charlie tried to land the giant fish.   [ ] Charlie woke up by the sound of waves crashing.

   [ ] Charlie tied his fishing line to the horse team.   [ ] Charlie waited for three days.

3. Check the box that tells what happened first.

   [ ] The cod lay on the river bank.   [ ] The level of the river dropped.

   [ ] Charlie unpacked his cart.

4. Charlie caught a fish on the second day he went fishing.   True [ ]   False [ ]

5. It took Charlie two days to get the fish out of the river.   True [ ]   False [ ]

6. Circle the words that tell you when Charlie finally caught his fish.

   (A) just as the sun was rising   (B) early hours of the morning   (C) at sunset

7. How many days total did Charlie spend catching his fish? More than _____ days

Name: _____   Date: _____

NUMBERING EXERCISES

Below are five sets of statements from various books. Can you put each set of statements in order? Number the boxes 1, 2, and 3 to show the order of events.

1. *The Day My Friend Learned to Dance* by Hazel Edwards

☐ I nodded, and he followed me.

☐ Jason looked uncomfortable. "Is it okay if we go in?" he whispered.

☐ Mom and Dad were behind us.

2. *Your Backyard Jungle* by Kerrie Bingle, David Bowden, and Jenny Dibley

☐ In some species, the female keeps the eggs in her body and produces live young.

☐ Young insects grow and develop in three different ways.

☐ All insects begin life as an egg.

3. *Mitsina, the Hermit* by David Shapiro

☐ Long ago, before men and women lived on Earth, gods and goddesses lived in heaven.

☐ Sharp-sighted Mitsina was an evil god.

☐ But not all gods and goddesses were good.

These two are more difficult. Number the boxes 1 through 4 to show the order of events.

4. *Spooked!* by Errol Broome

☐ The boys' scalps prickled.

☐ The doors rattled again.

☐ They held their breath, waiting for something to happen.

☐ Surely something had moved inside the closet.

5. *Quiet Pony for Sale* by Mary Small

☐ When he was alone in the garden, he was afraid that Mrs. Jenkin's cat would creep up and then jump in his lap.

☐ Derek was afraid of animals.

☐ He was born unable to walk, so spent most of his time in a wheelchair.

☐ The first time it had happened he had screamed in terror at the cat.

Name: _____ Date: _____

BOAT BOY
by Hazel Edwards

"Tomorrow is another of our special days," said Mrs. Bramble.

Dieu was class monitor that week. As he stacked the books, he looked up at the calendar above the shelf.

Special days for Mrs. Bramble were circled in green marker.

Pet Day. Smiling, Dieu remembered how the children screamed when Lisa's lizard escaped. And then Mario's dog had a fight with Nguyen's cat. The cat leapt on top of the cupboard, and Dieu climbed up to get her.

Yellow Day. Everyone wore yellow clothes and yellow face paint. They ate pumpkin scones with apricot jam.

Pioneer Day. Everyone wore shady hats, old trousers and big shirts. They ate bread and drank milk.

"Tomorrow is Grandparents' Day," said Mrs. Bramble.

"Bring along your grandparents. Remember those invitations you drew last week?"

Dieu remembered. On the way home, he had thrown his away. His grandmother wouldn't be coming.

Perhaps he could pretend to be sick tomorrow? But Mom wouldn't let him stay at home alone.

---

1. Draw a line to match the number and event, showing the order in which things happened.

First   The children screamed when Lisa's lizard escaped.

Second   Mrs. Bramble reminded the class to bring their grandparents.

Third   The class drew invitations.

Fourth   Dieu threw his invitation away.

2. What was the next special day going to be? _____

_____

3. Number the boxes 1 through 3 to show the order in which Mrs. Bramble said things.

☐ Mrs. Bramble said, "Tomorrow is another of our special days."

☐ Mrs. Bramble said, "Remember those invitations you drew last week?"

☐ Mrs. Bramble said, "Tomorrow is Grandparents' Day."

4. Instead of going to school, Dieu was going to help a cat.   True ☐

False ☐

Name: _____   Date: _____

A NIGHT AT BENNY'S

by Dianne Bates

(**Note:** The person who tells the story/poem is often called the *narrator* if we don't know his or her name.)

The night I was allowed to stay at Benny's place, my sister Fiona put up a terrible fuss.

"It's not fair!" she whined. "How come I have to stay home and do the washing up, while Brian gets to go to the new neighbors' place?"

Dad told her to pipe down, but she wouldn't.

"You always get out of things!" she bellowed, as I crammed my scout knife, football cards, and comics into the overnight bag. Dad bellowed back that she could wash and dry the dishes if she didn't do as she was told. When Benny and I left for next door, she was up to her elbows in soapsuds. "I'll get you!" she hissed at me.

"Fang Face!" I mouthed back.

A stream of soapsuds, aimed at me, hit Dad on the back of the neck. "For that, you can do the drying too," I heard him yell as Benny and I slammed the door behind us.

"If you think she's bad," said Benny, "wait till you meet Creep Features."

---

1. What was the first thing Fiona did to upset her father? _____

   _____

2. Draw a line to match the number with an event to show the order in which things happened.

   First   Dad was hit with a stream of soapsuds.

   Second   The narrator packs his overnight bag.

   Third   The narrator and Benny slammed the door.

   Fourth   Fiona was told not to complain.

3. Why did Dad yell at Fiona the first time? _____

   _____

4. Why did Dad yell at Fiona the second time? _____

   _____

5. When Fiona was told to wash up, Benny decided to help her.   True ☐   False ☐

6. Benny thought Fiona was worse than Creep Features.   True ☐   False ☐

7. Draw a circle around the word that tell us when Fiona began complaining.

   morning   noon   afternoon   night

Name: _____   Date: _____

HO, HO, HO!
by Jan Weeks

A week before Christmas, on a wintry night,
Snow lay around like a blanket of white.
The air was bitter, colder than ice
And no one went out without thinking twice.
Then, all of a sudden, a voice thundered out
Piercing the silence that lay all about.
It shouted so loud, so sharp and so clear,
That voice was meant for the whole world to hear.

Booming from somewhere up in the North Pole,
The voice said, "My pants have sprung a huge hole!
You could park a gigantic battleship there!
It's against the law—a crime, do you hear?
For a man like me to be exposed, dear!
How can I possibly go, 'Ho, ho, ho!'
With my underpants all out on show?"

Circle the word that completes each sentence.

1. The weather was (stormy   windy   cold) when Santa shouted.

2. A (day   week   month) before Christmas, Santa made an embarrassing discovery.

3. The hole was in Santa's (pants   underpants   North Pole).

4. In the poem, Santa is (most   a little   not) worried about battleships.

5. Number the boxes 1 through 3 to show the order of events.

☐ The weather had turned very cold.

☐ The silence was broken by a booming voice.

☐ Santa discovered a hole.

6. Draw a circle around the word that tells when the incident took place.

summer   autumn   winter   spring

7. In the poem, Santa doesn't feel he can celebrate Christmas.   True ☐   False ☐

8. Santa wanted to keep the hole in his pants a secret.   True ☐   False ☐

9. Everyone wanted to go out and enjoy the snow.   True ☐   False ☐

Name: _____   Date: _____

INTRODUCTION

You might have already read the following story, in which you practiced finding facts. Now let's read *Shiner* to try using **context clues**.

Sometimes, when we read, we are not always directly told all the information. Often we can work out what is happening, how people feel or where the action is by information in the writing. The context can also give clues to the meaning of new words.

Read this short passage.

> Andy peered at the street sign and shook his head. He tried to read the strange letters. Suddenly turning, he retraced his steps across the cold park. He had never been so cold in all his life. The park lights would soon be all the comfort he had.

Using context clues, we get two clues about Andy's situation: he is in a foreign place (couldn't read the strange letters) and night was approaching (the park lights are on). We also get the idea that he was not really prepared for the cold. We get this information from the context in which it appears.

Read this passage from *Shiner* by Marilyn Cosgrove.

A bull terrier is not everyone's idea of a good-looking dog, but Pat and George thought their new puppy was beautiful.

They lived in a new house and they meant her to be an outside dog, but the puppy decided that their bedroom was the place to sleep. No hot water bottles or ticking clocks would comfort this puppy. She just wanted to be near George and Pat.

A few restless nights soon turned into nights of contentment.

Pat and George found it hard to choose a name for this smiling bull terrier with the black eye-patch. Then George, a part-time wrestler, came home one night with a black eye.

"What a shiner!" cried Pat as she helped him through the door. She laughed when she noticed the puppy's puzzled expression. From that moment on, "Shiner" was the perfect name for a bull terrier with one black eye!

1. What did Pat and George use to encourage the puppy to sleep outside?

    a. _____   b. _____

2. The word "contentment" suggests that the nights were (enjoyable   noisy). (Circle one word.)

3. From the way George and Pat behave, we can tell that they are

  ☐ uncaring.   ☐ determined.   ☐ lonely.   ☐ soft-hearted.

4. The phrase "puzzled expression" suggests that Shiner was (pleased   confused   hungry). (Circle one word.)

Answers:
1. a. hot water bottles b. ticking clocks 2. enjoyable 3. soft-hearted. 4. confused

Name: _____   Date: _____

PETS' DAY
by Celeste Sowden

WHO: Miss Wilson (a student teacher)   Mrs. Brown (the class teacher)
         The Children (Matthew, Wendy, Tran, Joey, Soula, Jeremy, Lucy, Laura, Peter)
WHERE: An elementary school classroom
WHEN: Scene 1—Late afternoon   Scene 2—Early the following morning

Scene 1

Miss Wilson: Mrs. Brown, do you know what I'd like to do tomorrow for one of my lessons?

Mrs. Brown: No, Miss Wilson. What?

Miss Wilson: I'd like to teach the children about caring and sharing. I think caring and sharing is so important, don't you?

Mrs. Brown: Indeed, I do. And how are you going to care and share in one half-hour lesson, might I ask?

Miss Wilson: Well, I have an idea. May I put it to the class?

Mrs. Brown: You may. Listen, everyone. Miss Wilson has something important to say to us. Are you listening, Jeremy? Are we all listening? Peter, get down from the top of that cupboard. Ready? All right, Miss Wilson.

Miss Wilson: Well, children, what's the most important thing to do if you have a pet?

Matthew: Teach it how to fight.

Miss Wilson: Well, not quite . . .

Wendy: Train it to eat the scraps.

Miss Wilson: That's not really what I meant.

Tran: Get a newspaper if it wets on the carpet.

Miss Wilson: No. We have to c-c-c—

Joey: Carry it around?

---

1. Which word is Miss Wilson trying to get from the class when she says "c-c-c —"?

☐ carry   ☐ care   ☐ cut   ☐ control

2. The answers the children give Miss Wilson suggest that the children are

☐ responsible.   ☐ thinking.   ☐ considerate.   ☐ forgetful.

3. Miss Wilson was teaching a lesson in Mrs. Brown's class because

☐ she was getting teaching experience.   ☐ Mrs. Brown wanted to learn about pets.

☐ she was the school principal.   ☐ Miss Wilson's ideas always worked.

4. How would you describe the children in Miss Brown's class? _____

5. We know Peter was being naughty because he was _____ .

Name: _____   Date: _____

ALBERT'S BIRTHDAY

by Joan Dalgleish

"Missy? Missy, where are you?"

Albert stood still and listened. Nothing. No barks or whimpers; only the sound of the traffic on the road outside.

"I suppose you're taking a nap, old girl," he said as he shuffled slowly out to the kitchen to put the kettle on for his morning cup of tea. He lit the gas and sat down to wait for the water to boil. Albert ran his hand through his thin, white hair.

"We're not as young as we used to be, are we, girl? Why, I'll be eighty very soon. Never thought I'd make it. Not after that nasty flu I had last year. Eighty, not out, eh?" He chuckled, and wheezed into a cough. "Well, Missy, if I'm eighty then you must be fifteen. What's that in dog years? Let me see … seven years of my life equals one of yours. That's … that's …"

He tried to do the sum in his head, but it didn't want to be done. "Never was much good at mental arithmetic. I need a pencil and paper."

Albert's old bones creaked as he got up and went over to the telephone table. He picked up the pad and pencil he kept there for writing messages. The pad was blank because the phone hardly ever rang.

---

1. Give two examples that suggest to the reader that Albert was in poor health.

   a) _____   b) _____

2. Which of the following sentences suggests that Albert was lonely?

   ☐ The message pad was blank.   ☐ Missy did not come when she was called.

   ☐ Albert had thin white hair.   ☐ Sums were difficult for Albert.

3. In what part of the day is Albert thinking about the dog's age? _____

4. The phrase "wheezed into a cough" suggests that Albert was

   (having trouble breathing   breathing deeply   exhausted). (Circle one answer.)

5. From information in the story, it is most likely that Albert lives

   ☐ in the city.   ☐ near the sea.

   ☐ on a farm.   ☐ out in the country.

6. Albert was very good at working things out in his head.   True ☐

                                                              False ☐

7. Albert had a cup of tea every morning.   True ☐

                                             False ☐

DRAGONS OF CHINA

by Ida Chionh

Dragons in Myth

Where did they come from?

Some say that dragons are a creation of the imagination. Others say that they were real creatures which lived in harmony with humanity, many centuries ago.

In one legend, the first dragon came out of a great storm and tamed the floods by digging ditches, dykes, and canals.

In another legend, the dragon grew inside a large egg, which lay at the bottom of the sea for a thousand years. When it floated to the surface, its bright colors attracted someone to pick it up and bring it to land. There it lay for another thousand years.

At last the egg hatched, and the baby dragon immediately grew to an enormous size. It caused a great storm and flew up into heaven.

In Chinese mythology, there are five kinds of dragons, and each performs a different task.

The spiritual dragon controls the wind and rain.

The earthly dragon marks the course of rivers and deepens the seas.

The celestial dragon guards and supports the mansions of the gods in heaven.

The guardian dragon keeps treasure hidden from **mortal** eyes.

The imperial dragon protects the emperor and his household.

Two of these dragons have a special importance in Chinese mythology: the spiritual dragon and the imperial dragon.

---

1. If we say dragons are a "creation of the imagination," we mean they

☐ exist nowhere but in people's minds.   ☐ exist in some countries and not others.

☐ lived a time a long time ago.   ☐ may exist, but it hasn't been proven.

2. One story about a dragon suggests that, at first, it

☐ hatched from an egg that laid on the land for a thousand years.   ☐ hatched very quickly.

☐ came to the earth from rainbows.   ☐ hatched in groups of five.

3. Which dragon controls the winds? _____

4. The word "celestial" refers to things that happen in the heavens.

True ☐   False ☐

5. The word "imperial" refers to things from the imagination.

True ☐   False ☐

6. The word "mortal" could be replaced with (human   seeing   ancient). (Circle one word.)

JACK FINDS THE OUTBACK

by Judith Womersley

"What is the outback?" Jack used to ask. "Where is it? What does it look like?"

He imagined it to be a big space out beyond Dad's backyard. But that couldn't be quite the right explanation, he knew, because behind Dad's house there were other houses and behind them, high-rise apartments. Jack could see them from the upstairs bedroom where he always slept when he stayed with his father.

Dad explained that the outback was a huge space in the middle of Australia.

"Are there people there?" Jack asked.

"Not many," Dad said. "It's mainly sand and saltbush."

"Does saltbush taste salty?"

Jack's dad laughed and said, "I don't know, son. I've never tasted it."

"Are there animals there?" asked Jack.

"Oh, yes," said Dad. "Lots of animals— kangaroos and wallabies and emus and wild cats and cattle …"

"Any snakes?" asked Jack.

"Some," said his father, "but not enough to worry about."

And then Jack would always ask the question that **puzzled** him the most, "Where does the outback begin?"

---

1. Find two examples in the story that suggest that the outback is a bit like the desert.

   a) _____   b)_____

2. From the questions Jack asks, you would say he was

   ☐ rude.   ☐ inquisitive.

   ☐ foolish.   ☐ nosy.

3. It is most likely Jack has been to the outback.   True ☐   False ☐

4. The word "puzzled" could be replaced by "bewildered."   True ☐   False ☐

5. The outback began behind the high-rise apartments.   True ☐   False ☐

6. Jack's father knew about wild animals in the outback.   True ☐   False ☐

THE DAY MY FRIEND LEARNED TO DANCE

by Hazel Edwards

"Do you want to come to a barbecue on Sunday, Jason? It's a Macedonian picnic."

Our class was getting changed for T-ball. I waited for Jason to say no.

My mom said I had to ask him. And when Mom's made up her mind, you don't argue.

"Jason asked you to his birthday party," she said. "You must ask him to Saint Naum Ohridski's Monastery picnic."

What Mom doesn't know is that Jason asked the whole class to his party. She was just so pleased that I was invited.

Mom doesn't understand. Jason was born here. He plays Aussie Rules, not soccer. He eats hamburgers, not savory pastries like maznik or **zelnik**. When we had to fill in the form for Mr. Burgess about religious instruction classes, Jason left it blank. Jason goes to discos, not Macedonian dancing classes.

I'm the expert on dancing classes. I'm the only Macedonian kid who's had 56 lessons and still can't dance.

---

1. About how old do you think Jason is? _____

2. What makes you think he is that old? _____

_____

3. If you had some zelnik, you would (eat it   cook with it). (Circle one answer.)

4. The phrase "when Mom's made up her mind, you don't argue" suggests that

☐ Mom had many arguments.   ☐ Mom didn't care what happened.

☐ people did what they were told.   ☐ it took Mom a long time to make up her mind.

5. What is another good title for this story?_____

6. The narrator invited Jason to the picnic while they were at

☐ school.   ☐ the narrator's place.

☐ a barbecue.   ☐ a football game.

7. In the story, the narrator could best be described as (happy   angry   uneasy). (Circle one answer.)

8. The narrator felt special because he was invited to Jason's party.   True ☐

False ☐

9. After 56 lessons, the narrator had become an expert dancer.   True ☐

False ☐

Name: _____   Date: _____

INTRODUCTION

You might have already read part of the following story, in which you practiced using context clues. Now let's read *Albert's Birthday* to try **drawing conclusions**.

Drawing conclusions is an advanced reading skill. It requires you to make a judgment about what you have read. It requires that you can find the main idea (page 14), can use context clues (page 28), have dictionary skills (page 58) and can draw upon other reading skills.

A conclusion is reached by reasoning (thinking about a situation). It may require you to have an opinion or make a decision. Drawing conclusions can only be done after you have read the whole extract (or story)—when you have all the information.

Read this story from *Albert's Birthday* by Joan Dalgleish.

"Missy? Missy, where are you?"

Albert stood still and listened. Nothing. No barks or whimpers; only the sound of the traffic on the road outside.

"I suppose you're taking a nap, old girl," he said as he shuffled slowly out to the kitchen to put the kettle on for his morning cup of tea. He lit the gas and sat down to wait for the water to boil. Albert ran his hand through his thin, white hair.

"We're not as young as we used to be, are we, girl? Why, I'll be eighty very soon. Never thought I'd make it. Not after that nasty flu I had last year. Eighty, not out,

eh?" He chuckled, and wheezed into a cough. "Well, Missy, if I'm eighty then you must be fifteen. What's that in dog years? Let me see … seven years of my life equals one of yours. That's … that's …"

He tried to do the sum in his head, but it didn't want to be done. "Never was much good at mental arithmetic. I need a pencil and paper."

Albert's old bones creaked as he got up and went over to the telephone table. He picked up the pad and pencil he kept there for writing messages. The pad was blank, because the phone hardly ever rang.

1. Albert is old but he is not a sad person. List some of the things Albert does that help you draw this conclusion. _____

_____

2. What details help you draw the conclusion that Albert was not worried about Missy? (Give two examples.)

a. _____   b. _____

3. Albert could be described as (easily upset   messy   contented). (Circle one answer.)

4. Another good title for this story would be (Old Friends   Catching the Flu). (Circle one answer.)

Answers:

1. Possible answers: He is content that he has had a long life, or he accepts his limitations, or he has a pet dog that he cares for. 2. He didn't go looking for her; he found things to laugh about. 3. contented 4. Old Friends

CHARLIE'S FISH AND OTHER TALES

by R. L. Muddyman

You might have already read one of the tales, in which you practiced sequencing. Now read *Charlie's Fish and Other Tales* to try drawing conclusions.

Gold Fever—A Tale by Bill the Bushy

"I carefully dropped my nuggets into an old sock, tying a knot so they wouldn't fall out. Then I headed off to town to sell my find. I went to a gold buyer I knew I could trust, and when I tipped the nuggets out on the table, his eyes nearly popped out of his head. You wouldn't believe what he told me."

"It appears that the day before I arrived, one of the mining companies had been blasting just upriver from where I was camped. One of the charges hadn't gone off when it was supposed to. Well, the boss hadn't counted properly, so he thought the blasting was over. When he gave the all clear, the miners started back to work. Just as they reached the diggings, the last charge exploded, knocking them off their feet!"

"Luckily, no one was hurt, but the explosion was so loud that it blew all the gold fillings out of their mouths and into the creek. It seems that these gold fillings were the nuggets I had found."

"Well, I thought I should do the right thing, so I took my old sock and went down to the diggings. Sure enough, when the miners saw the gold, each man recognized his own filling and popped it back into his mouth, where it belonged."

1. Circle the letters of the details that help you draw the conclusion that this tale may not be true.

   (A) Bill put his nuggets in an old sock.   (D) The miners recognized their gold fillings.

   (B) Bill went to town to sell his gold.   (E) The men were mining near a river.

   (C) The explosion knocked the miners' fillings out of their mouths.

2. What information leads you to the conclusion that the gold buyer was surprised by

   Bill's nuggets? _____

3. Bill the Bushy could best be described as a (comedian   liar). (Circle one answer.) Which of these details help you draw this conclusion?

   ☐ Bill gave the gold back to the owners.   ☐ Bill's story is a tall tale.

   ☐ Bill is trying to make people laugh.   ☐ The miners were expecting Bill.

   ☐ Bill blames the boss for the explosion.   ☐ The gold buyer was amazed.

4. Give a detail from the story that helps you draw the conclusion that it is not true. _____

   _____

   _____

DRAWING CONCLUSIONS

Name: _____   Date: _____

JOANNE
by Paul Williams

You might have already read part of the following story, in which you practiced finding the main idea. Now read *Joanne* to try drawing conclusions.

The weeks that followed were exciting. Joanne and Dad explored together. They had decided to move to the country, and the weekends were spent searching for their new home. They didn't have much luck at first. They found plenty of nice towns, but no jobs.

Then one day Graham arrived with a letter from his son Peter. Peter owned a dairy farm in a country town. He wanted to sell it and move back to the city. At last, a change of luck! Dad would buy the dairy farm, and they would move to the country.

Joanne stayed with Graham and his wife Maree, while Dad organized the move and settled into his new job. He boarded with a friend of Peter's. Milk deliveries began at 5 in the morning and were usually finished by 2:30 P.M. Then Dad would drive around the district searching for a house to buy.

Most nights, he telephoned Joanne. He always asked Joanne about school, but she was more interested in what he had been doing.

One night, during dinner, the phone rang and Joanne answered it.

"Hello, little one. What's new?"

Joanne could sense the excitement in his voice.

1. Which of these details helps you draw the conclusion that Joanne's dad had some good news?

   (A) searching for a house   (B) decided to move to the country

   (C) deliveries began at 5   (D) excitement in his voice

   (E) most nights he telephones Joanne   (F) Joanne and Dad explored together

2. What detail helps you draw the conclusion that Dad worked hard? _____

_____

_____

3. Joanne (was   was not) in regular contact with her father. (Circle the choice.)

   Which detail helps you draw this conclusion?

   ☐ Dad stayed with Graham.   ☐ Dad asked Joanne about school.

   ☐ Most nights Dad telephoned.   ☐ Dad was searching for a house.

   ☐ Dad finished work at 2:30 P.M.   ☐ Dad's luck changed.

4. Circle the words that describe Joanne's dad.

   crafty   careless   dedicated   lazy   wealthy   determined

QUIET PONY FOR SALE

by Mary Small

You might have already read part of the following story, in which you practiced finding the main idea and sequencing events. Now read *Quiet Pony for Sale* to try drawing conclusions.

On the following Tuesday morning a small group of excited children set out in the school minibus for their first riding lesson. Derek and his mother went too.

The riding school was in a valley, close to semi-desert. The children peered out of the windows as the bus came along the track to the stables. There, standing in a row waiting for them, were the ponies! There were a lot of people, too. They were helpers who had come to make sure that the children rode safely. They came forward to greet the riders.

"All the ponies are very quiet," said Mrs. Harvey, the riding instructor. "They were specially chosen. Now, all of you come over here, and we'll find hard hats to fit everyone."

The children giggled as the riding hats were tried on for size. All except Derek. He clung to his mother.

"We are only sitting on the ponies today," said Mrs. Harvey. "Come on, Derek. Don't you want to try?"

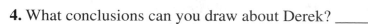

1. The children were thrilled to have a riding lesson. Circle the words that help you draw this conclusion.

   (A) excited   (C) giggled   (E) minibus

   (B) Tuesday   (D) valley   (F) people

2. What detail helps you draw the conclusion that Derek didn't want to join in the lesson?

_____

3. Which details help you draw the conclusion that the riding school makes the children feel welcome?

   (A) The ponies were all very quiet.

   (B) The children were greeted when they arrived.

   (C) The riding school had the ponies ready.

   (D) Derek's mother went with the children on the bus.

   (E) Mrs. Harvey encouraged the children to join in.

4. What conclusions can you draw about Derek? _____

_____

5. Mrs. Harvey was a (**bossy**   kind   sad   **strict**) person. (Circle one answer.)

6. Mrs. Harvey was (**well-prepared**   disorganized   unsure   worried). (Circle one answer.)

Name: _____   Date: _____

BOBBY BOY

by Errol Broome

You might have already read part of the following passage, in which you practiced finding facts and finding the main idea. Now read *Bobby Boy* to try drawing conclusions.

When the champion was five, he had grown even bigger. He was a giant who could win any race asked of him, a giant who might become the greatest horse in the world.

No other horse could get near him. To give them a chance, Phar Lap was asked to carry more and more weight. Most jockeys weigh around 50 kilograms, yet Phar Lap started in the 1931 Melbourne Cup with a load of 68 kilograms on his back.

For the third year in a row, Phar Lap was favorite for the event, but, on the day before the race, stories spread that he was not well. He had won eight races in nine weeks and had carried 56 kilograms or more every time. Two days before the Cup, he had won a four-horse race by only half a length. He was tired, perhaps not quite himself.

Now Phar Lap faced what the newspapers called "a stupendous task." Surely no horse could carry that weight to victory. Although Phar Lap ran well for a time, he faded in the straight and dropped back through the field. Tommy watched with tears in his eyes as his Bobby Boy (Phar Lap) struggled to the post. Sick and exhausted, Phar Lap finished eighth. He had carried 25 kilograms more than the winner.

That was Phar Lap's last race in Australia. After a visit to his birthplace, New Zealand, he was off to conquer the world.

---

1. Circle the letters next to the facts that help you draw the conclusion that Phar Lap was a very unusual horse.

   (A) He won eight races in nine weeks.   (C) He ran in the 1931 Melbourne Cup.

   (B) He had his name in the newspaper.   (D) He carried more weight than any other horse in the race.

2. Describe how Tommy felt after the race. _____

3. Phar Lap crossed the 1931 Cup finish line (with   without) difficulty. (Circle the answer.)

4. Draw a check in the box next to the details that make this a reasonable conclusion?

   ☐ Phar Lap had won many races.   ☐ Phar Lap carried 68 kilograms in the race.

   ☐ Phar Lap had won a race two   ☐ Phar Lap was favorite to win the race.
       days earlier.

5. What detail helps you draw the conclusion that, even though Phar Lap finished eighth in the 1931 Cup, his trainer still expected Phar Lap to be a great racehorse?

Name: _____   Date: _____

SHINER
by Marilyn Cosgrove

You might have already read part of the following story, in which you practiced finding facts and using context clues. Now read *Shiner* to try drawing conclusions.

The next day, the sun was shining at last. George rented a machine to dig out some steps up to the house. Pat stood watching, enjoying the long awaited sunshine.

A family had just moved into the vacant house next door. When her new neighbor walked out on to the balcony, Pat called, "I hope the noise isn't worrying you."

"No, it's fine, although I didn't sleep much last night. I thought there was a cat on the balcony, so I put out a saucer of milk, but the noise kept on. I slept with a pillow over my head all night."

"I know the feeling," said Pat. "My husband and I haven't slept well for three weeks, since we lost our dog."

"That's strange that you should mention a dog. Just as I walked along the hallway, I heard the same noise again and wondered if there was a dog under our house."

"George!" Pat let out a shriek that echoed throughout the neighborhood, and George nearly fell off the machine. He came running.

"Get a flashlight!" he yelled.

George clambered up the steep path to a small, open trapdoor, which led into the blackness under the house next door.

---

1. Which of these details help you draw the conclusion that the neighbor was a friendly person?

   (A) The neighbor objected to George digging up the steps.

   (B) The neighbor complained that he had been kept awake all night.

   (C) The neighbor did not like cats making a noise.

   (D) The neighbor was understanding about the loss of the dog.

   (E) The neighbor didn't protest about the work George was doing.

2. Draw a line to match the person with what they did.

   The neighbor   wanted a flashlight to look under the house.

   George   was first to realize where the dog might be.

   Pat   put out a saucer of milk for the stray cat.

What details help you conclude that George and Pat were thrilled that they might find their dog?

3. Pat: _____

4. George: _____

5. You can conclude that the neighbor had a cat and dog of his own.   True ☐   False ☐

Name: _____   Date: _____

INTRODUCTION

You might have already read part of the following story, in which you practiced using context clues and drawing conclusions. Now let's read *Albert's Birthday* to try **noting details**.

Details play an important part in written works. They help give the reader a clear understanding of the story or the topic. Details can give different types of writing its particular flavor and often allow the reader to draw conclusions. (See page 34.)

Read this story from *Albert's Birthday* by Joan Dalgleish.

> After tea and toast, Albert went into the backyard. Missy often pushed out through the flap in the back door and went to lie in the small patch of sun that came between the gap in the tall buildings surrounding the garden. She was not there.
>
> He opened the door to the space underneath the house. Still Missy did not answer his call. It was very strange.

We read that Albert is looking for his dog, Missy. The detail gives us some understanding of the type of person Albert is.

1. What details suggest that Albert cares about Missy? _____

_____

_____

2. What detail suggests that Albert lives in a suburb where there are lots of people?

_____

3. What details suggest that this incident took place in the morning? _____

_____

Read another passage from *Albert's Birthday* by Joan Dalgleish.

> At lunch on Thursday, Albert began to get ready. He pressed his brown pants, ironed his striped shirt and shined his shoes. He searched through his chest of drawers for his best sweater. It smelled of moth balls, but a walk in the open air would soon fix that.

4. What actions tell the reader that Albert had something special to do on this day?

_____

5. What details tell the reader that Albert had not worn his sweater for a quite a while?

_____

Answers:
1. The details that tell the reader that Albert cares are: the flap in the door so Missy can come and go whenever she likes; Albert's search around the yard for Missy; Albert knows Missy's habits well (where she lies to enjoy the sun). 2. Possible answer: The house is surrounded by tall buildings. 3. Albert has just had tea and toast for breakfast; the sun was not high in the sky; Missy may have left the house before Albert got up to get some morning sun. 4. He took a lot of care in getting his clothes ready. 5. Albert had to search for his sweater. It was probably in the bottom of the drawer. It had been in moth balls. Some people do this to keep moths away from their clothes if they aren't going to wear them for a long time.

Name: _____   Date: _____

THE STORY OF CAMELS IN AUSTRALIA

by Keren Lavelle

The Newcomers

For the past two centuries, people from many other parts of the world have come to live in Australia. These people brought with them many plants and animals that now live in Australia. We call these plants and animals introduced *species*.

People brought animals to Australia for a number of reasons.

Animals like sheep, cattle, and pigs were brought here to be farmed.

Animals like horses and bulls were brought here to transport people and goods.

Some animals, like cats and dogs, were brought to Australia as pets.

Animals that have been tamed by people are known as *domestic animals*.

Some animals, like rabbits and foxes, were brought here so that people could hunt them for sport. In Britain, wealthy people hunted these animals, and some settlers wanted to be able to do the same in Australia.

Some animals, like rats and mice, came here uninvited, as stowaways on ships.

---

1. Draw a line to match the detail that goes with each animal.

horses	sport
pigs	transport
foxes	pets
cats	food

2. How did introduced animals and plants come into Australia? _____

_____

Write short answers for these questions.

3. What do we call animals that have been tamed? _____

4. How did mice come to Australia? _____

5. According to the passage, what are three introduced animals? a) _____

  b) _____   c) _____

Complete these sentences, using the words in the passage.

6. People brought animals and _____ to Australia for a number of reasons. They brought pigs and _____ to provide food. Horses could be used for hunting, but they were also used to _____ . Rats came to Australia as stowaways on the _____ that also brought people.

Name: _____   Date: _____

DINKY-DI
by Shane Power

When the new arrivals came to Australia, they brought with them expressions that were to become part of a new language in their new life in a strange, new country.

Many were convicts, who came from different parts of Britain and Ireland. Life was sometimes hard in the poorer parts of these lands. It was important to keep a sense of fun, and this often showed itself in the language of the people. The expressions they used were humorous and colorful.

Many convicts were people who had little or no education in their own country. They did not have the opportunity to learn how to read or write. So they relied on the spoken word for communication. Most of the language they heard was slang, so that is what they copied in their own speech.

Some of the early settlers spoke in the same way. Others spoke differently because they came from different areas—north, south, east, and west. The new settlers introduced words and sayings never heard before on this side of the world. A great deal of the early language used in Australia was slang, and Australians are still famous for their use of these lively expressions.

The new Australians had to invent new slang words because this was a different country. They were seeing new flora and fauna. They were living in a strange climate and experiencing a whole new way of life. This country was not like their old home. They did not have the words to describe a lot of their new experiences. But by combining their old slang with some new slang, a whole new dinky-di language was invented.

1. Draw a line to match the details that go together.

strange land	lively expressions
hard life	humorous expressions
modern Australians	new expressions

2. Choose the best way to complete this sentence.

   Many of the convicts

   ☐ communicated by reading and writing.   ☐ used slang from their homelands to communicate.

   ☐ took a long time to learn Australian slang.

3. All convicts came from the same place.   True ☐   False ☐

4. Many convicts used a lot of slang because that's all they heard.   True ☐   False ☐

5. Settlers came from different places and used different expressions.   True ☐   False ☐

6. Today, Australians are well known for their colorful expressions.   True ☐   False ☐

7. The early settlers were well prepared for their new life in Australia.   True ☐   False ☐

Name: _____   Date: _____

TV NEWS
by Elizabeth Halley

An Interview with Geraldine Doogue (TV News Reporter)

EH: What happens after you've had your make-up and hair done?

GD: I come downstairs and do what's called a *promo*. It's a short advertisement for what's coming on the news that night, and we prerecord that in the studio. At Channel Ten our studio is our newsroom —we've set it up with lights and the camera positioned so that you can see the studio in the middle of a working newsroom. We record four promos: one to air at four-thirty, for thirty seconds, one to air at five o'clock, for thirty seconds, one at five thirty, for about thirty seconds, and one at about five to six that just says "coming up next."

EH: And on these promos do you outline what the main news items are?

GD: It's not like the news. You tease the viewers. Promos are like little advertisements. You let people know what the main stories are, saying, "Please watch us—you'd be crazy to miss this."

EH: Who writes the promos?

GD: One of the writers on the desk—there are usually two or three writers. They also write the scripts for the main news.

EH: And who picks out the film that you use?

GD: There's a pool of *editors* who actually choose the material.

---

1. Draw a line to match the details that go together.

editors   main news

promo   news advertisement

scripts   select the film for the news

2. News reporters get their make-up done in the studio.   True ☐   False ☐

3. Promos last for about one hour.   True ☐   False ☐

4. The news reporter has to prepare thirty to forty promos.   True ☐   False ☐

5. Promos provide the viewer with full news reports.   True ☐   False ☐

6. At Channel Ten the studio is used as the newsroom.   True ☐   False ☐

7. Name two items written by the writers.

   a) _____   b) _____

8. The make-up room is (beside   above   under) the newsroom. (Circle one answer.)

Name: _____ Date: _____

A NIGHT AT BENNY'S
by Dianne Bates

You might have already read the following story, in which you practiced sequencing. Now read *A Night at Benny's* to try noting details. (**Note:** The person who tells the story/poem is often called the *narrator* if we don't know his or her name.)

The night I was allowed to stay at Benny's place, my sister Fiona put up a terrible fuss.

"It's not fair!" she whined. "How come I get to stay home and do the washing up, while Brian gets to go to the new neighbors' place?"

Dad told her to pipe down, but she wouldn't.

"You always get out of things!" she bellowed, as I crammed my scout knife, football cards, and comics into the overnight bag. Dad bellowed back that she could wash and dry the dishes if she didn't do as she was told. When Benny and I left for next door, she was up to her elbows in soapsuds. "I'll get you!" she hissed at me.

"Fang Face!" I mouthed back.

A stream of soapsuds, aimed at me, hit Dad on the back of the neck. "For that you can do the drying, too," I heard him yell as Benny and I slammed the door behind us.

"If you think she's bad," said Benny, "wait till you meet Creep Features."

I met Creep Features, alias Felicity, about half an hour later. Benny and I were trampolining on his bed when the door flew open.

---

1. Draw a line to match the person with an important detail.

Felicity   throws soapsuds at Brian (the narrator)

Benny   nickname is Creep Features

Fiona   tells Fiona to wash and dry the dishes

Dad   uses the bed as a trampoline

2. Number the boxes 1, 2, and 3 to show the order in which Brian did things.

☐ teased Fiona   ☐ got invited to Benny's place   ☐ packed his bag

3. Benny thought that Fiona was worse than Felicity.   True ☐   False ☐

4. Brian packed his pajamas when he went to stay at Benny's place. True ☐   False ☐

5. Fiona and Brian were like (old friends   enemies   strangers). (Circle one answer.)

6. Brian felt (sorry   angry   smug   worried) when Fiona was told she had to wash up. (Circle one answer.)

7. Use the details from the story to describe Brian. _____

_____

8. What detail let's the reader know that Brian and Benny don't have far to go? _____

_____

IN THE MADE-UP WORLD

by Bill Condon

In the made-up world of Maurice Mouse,
He is the owner of the house.
He makes the rules which cats obey;
They wait on him, both night and day.

Cats bring him cheese and call him "Sir"
And ask permission before they purr.

If he decides to have some fun,
He'll scare a cat and make it run,
He'll chase it up a willow tree
And then he'll charge a rescue fee.

He has two cats to wash his cars
(One Mousemobile, three Rodent Stars)
And cats as well patrol the house —
Watchdog cats to guard a mouse!

He does not live in mouse-like quarters,
Nor do his wife or sons and daughters.

They live inside a cattery,
Where all they hear is flattery
From loyal feline followers
Who think the mouse supreme.

Oh, how Maurice Mouse
Hates waking from his dream!

Write short answers to these questions

1. What are the cats scared of? _____

2. What does Maurice Mouse call the house where he lives? _____

3. What do the cats ask permission to do? _____

4. How does Maurice Mouse have fun? _____

5. List three things the cats do for Maurice Mouse.   a. _____

　　　 b. _____   c. _____

6. Maurice Mouse lives all by himself.   True ☐   False ☐

7. The cats says nasty things about the mouse family.   True ☐   False ☐

8. Maurice Mouse hates waking up because _____

_____

9. Maurice Mouse's house is protected by

(A) patrol cars.   (C) watch dogs.

(B) other mice.   (D) cats.

Name: _____   Date: _____

INTRODUCTION

If we want to know how to do something we have to follow a procedure or, to use another term, **follow directions**. You may have books at home that tell you how to do things. They might be about how to make papier-mâché or how to bake a cake.

You will find many books that give directions in your school library: how to play a sport, how to do magic tricks, how to knit, how to do science experiments, how to recycle waste materials, and so on. Many magazines also give directions: recipes, do-it-yourself tips, and so on.

Some directions are simple. A sign on a railway station tells the passengers how to get a ticket from a ticket machine. We call each part of the directions, or instructions, steps.

Some directions have many steps. The directions for replacing a part in a car could be quite complex. People follow directions for something nearly every day of their lives.

Read the following set of simple instructions for how to make Peta Pea Soup from *Healthy Treats to Make and Eat* **by Eleanor Parker.**

Peta Pea Soup	— *the aim*
You will need:	
1 sliced carrot	— *the materials*
1 diced onion	*(or ingredients)*
2 sticks of celery, sliced	
½ turnip, diced	
½ cup dried split peas	
1 teaspoon cumin powder	
1 teaspoon vegetable stock or seasoning	
4 tablespoons alfalfa sprouts	
What to do:	
1. Soak the split peas in two cups of water overnight.	— *the steps*
2. Cook the split peas in 1 liter of boiling water for half an hour.	*(directions)*
3. Add seasonings and vegetables.	
4. When all the ingredients are soft, blend the soup to a puree.	
5. Serve hot.	— *concluding step*
Garnish each bowl of soup with a tablespoon of alfalfa sprouts.	— *concluding statement*

1. How many steps are there in making Peta Pea Soup? _____

2. How many different ingredients do you need for Peta Pea Soup? _____

3. What does this set of directions help you do? _____

_____

4. What should you add right before you serve Peta Pea Soup? _____

Answers:

1. five steps 2. eight 3. These directions help you make Peta Pea Soup. 4. alfalfa sprouts

BANANA DELIGHT ICE CREAM

You will need:
6 large ripe bananas
⅓ cup cold-pressed oil
2 tablespoons of honey
4 tablespoons milk powder
(cow or soy milk powder)
½ cup water
1 tablespoon lemon juice
½ cup carob chips

Steps:
1. Place all the ingredients in a blender and blend thoroughly.

2. When the mixture turns into a thick cream, pour it into a refrigerator container, cover and put into the freezer. It does not require a second beating.

You do not always need to serve this mixture frozen. It also tastes delicious poured over fruit, like cream.

Answer questions 1 through 3 with short answers.

1. How many different ingredients are needed to make Banana Delight Ice Cream? _____

2. How many steps in the instructions for making Banana Delight Ice Cream? _____

3. How many bananas are used when making Banana Delight Ice Cream? _____

4. Using your own words, what is the purpose of these instructions? _____

_____

Fill in the blanks to complete each of these sentences.

5. Put all the _____ in a blender and blend thoroughly.

6. After the mixture turns to a thick cream, _____ it in the freezer.

7. In Step 2, you should

☐ beat the mixture a second time.   ☐ wait until the mixture freezes before serving.

☐ pour the mixture over fruit.   ☐ put the mixture in a covered container.

8. To make Banana Delight Ice Cream, you will need 1 tablespoon of

☐ honey.   ☐ powdered milk.

☐ water.   ☐ lemon juice.

9. In this recipe, if you did not have cow's milk powder, you could use soy milk powder.

True ☐   False ☐

10. The <u>concluding statement</u> has a second way to serve the ice cream.

True ☐   False ☐

HOW TO BE A MAGICIAN

compiled by Rachael Collinson

The Well-Trained Ball Trick

Props:
★ table, covered with a cloth
★ 1 bangle bracelet or large curtain ring
★ 1 ping-pong ball
★ thread or fishing line

Preparation:
★ Set up the table so that the cloth hangs to the floor, except on the side in front of you.
★ Attach the bangle bracelet or curtain ring to a length of thread. The thread should be the same color as the tablecloth and a bit longer than the table.
★ Put the bangle bracelet or curtain ring under the tablecloth, with the thread dangling where you can grasp it easily without anyone seeing it.

The Act:
Placing a ping-pong ball in the center of the table, you tell your audience that this ball comes when it's called. You call to the ping-pong ball, "Come on, Henry, come when you're called!"
Look, the ping-pong ball moves towards you! You command it to stop, which it does. Then you call it again, and it comes towards you. "Come along, Henry!"

Performance:
★ Standing behind the table, place the ping-pong ball so that it sits inside the curtain ring or bangle bracelet.
★ Pull the thread down, so that the bangle bracelet or ring moves towards you with the ball inside it. Stop pulling, and the ball will stop moving.
Note: Practice pulling the thread gently and smoothly, without jerking it.

This is a different set of instructions. Answer questions 1 through 3 with short answers.

1. How many things do you need to perform this trick? _____

2. How many steps are there in the preparations, before doing the trick? _____

3. What can be used instead of a thread? _____

Fill in the blanks to complete the sentences for numbers 4 and 5.

4. As you _____ the trick, you should _____ to the audience.

5. The words to say to the audience are added to help make the trick seem like _____.

6. The ping pong ball can move forward and backwards.   True ☐   False ☐

7. Number the boxes 1 through 4 to show the order of the steps you would follow when doing the trick.

☐ Cover a table with a cloth.   ☐ Place the bangle bracelet under the tablecloth.

☐ Collect the props.   ☐ Tie a long thread to a bangle bracelet.

Name: _____   Date: _____

GROWING YOUR OWN SPROUTS
by Eleanor Parker

You will need:
- an empty jar
- a rubber band
- a piece of cheese cloth, nylon stocking, or gauze
- fresh sprout seeds

You can buy sprout seeds which have been specially mixed for sprouting. Alfalfa, mung beans, brown lentils, and fenugreek seeds make tasty sprouts. You can buy them in health food stores.

What to do:
1. Put a tablespoon of seeds in a jar. Cover the top of the jar with cloth and secure it tightly with a rubber band.
2. Half fill the jar with warm water and allow the seeds to stand in it for about two hours. After this, turn the jar upside down to drain the water. The cloth will stop the seeds from falling out.
3. Put the jar in a dark place (like a cupboard) overnight. This helps the seeds sprout faster.
4. The next day, bring the jar out into the light again.
5. Rinse the seeds in cold water twice a day (morning and evening) to keep them moist. Make sure you drain the water each time, otherwise the seeds will go slimy and moldy. Leave the seeds on top of a bench near a window, but not in the sunlight or they will dry out too quickly.
6. They are ready to eat when they have sprouted roots and green leaves and are about 30 mm to 50 mm long.
7. Give the sprouts a final rinse to remove the seed husks before you eat them.

Clean the jar with soap and hot water. Your jar is now ready for another crop of sprouts.

---

1. What is the first step in growing sprouts? _____

_____

2. What is in the first thing you put in the jar? _____

3. What is the final step before eating the sprouts? _____

_____

4. Number the boxes 1 through 4 to tell the order of the steps for growing sprouts.

☐ Put the seeds in the jar in a dark place.   ☐ Bring the seeds into the sunlight.

☐ Keep the seeds moist as they germinate.   ☐ Soak the seeds in warm water.

5. The rubber band is used to _____ .

6. If you didn't have cheese cloth you could use nylon.   True ☐   False ☐

Name: _____   Date: _____

INTRODUCTION

You might have already read part of this story, in which you practiced finding the main idea and drawing conclusions. Now let's read *Joanne* to try **understanding questions**.

In your comprehension exercises, you will answer many different types of questions. Different types of questions are used to see just how well you read and understand what you have read. You will get a number of different types of questions in this section.

Types of questions:

true–false questions (yes–no)	multiple-choice questions	short answer questions
answer with complete sentences	matching exercises	sentence completion exercises
sequencing questions	labelling exercises	cloze exercises

Questions that want you to find information may begin with *who, when, where,* or *what.* Sometimes you will be asked to give names or make lists.

Questions that want you to give a reason will often begin with *why.*

Some questions may ask you to give an opinion. For these questions, you have to express your own ideas. These questions will ask you to give answers in your own words.

Read this story from *Joanne* by Paul Williams and answer the questions.

But one day, tragedy struck. As Joanne left the school playground, she heard a siren. When she arrived home, she saw a crowd gathered around the pedestrian crossing in front of the general store. Just as she arrived at the crossing so did the ambulance. The police were already there.

Joanne pushed her way through the front of the crowd of onlookers.

Jack was lying on the road. Joanne's father was kneeling next to him, holding his hand. Scotty was lying next to Jack, licking his other hand. Both the boy and dog were bleeding.

1. Where did the accident happen? _____

_____

2. Draw a line to match the beginning of each sentence with its correct ending.

Joanne's father   were lying on the road.

Joanne was on her way home   was trying to comfort Jack.

Scotty and Jack   when she heard the siren.

3. Joanne was the first person to help Jack. True ☐ False ☐

4. Fill in the blanks to complete this sentence.

Joanne's father was _____ one of Jack's hands and Scotty was _____ the other hand.

Answers:

1. The accident happened at a pedestrian crossing in front of the general store. 2. Joanne's father/was trying to comfort Jack. Joanne was on her way home/when she heard the siren. Scotty and Jack/were lying on the road. 3. False 4. holding, licking

Name: _____   Date: _____

YOUR BACKYARD JUNGLE: PLANTS

by K. Bingle, D. Bowden and J Dibley

Algae

Algae mostly live in the water, both salt and fresh, and also in damp places on land. There are several kinds of algae. They are different shapes and different sizes. Seaweed and kelp are algae.

In your backyard, you may find green algae growing on the top of still water, such as a fishpond. Algae also grows on bricks and stones, making them slippery when wet.

Fungi

Fungi are a group of plants that cannot make their own food because they do not contain chlorophyll. Instead they feed on other plants or animals. Molds, yeasts, mushrooms, and toadstools are fungi.

Look for mushrooms and toadstools in your own backyard. They usually grow in damp places away from sunlight and often appear after a few days of heavy rain. They grow on dead or dying plant matter.

1. The following words go with algae or fungi. Write them under the correct heading.

kelp	mushrooms	yeast	salt water	toadstools
mold	seaweed	dead leaves	contains chlorophyll	fishpond

Algae   **Fungi**

_____   _____

_____   _____

_____   _____

_____   _____

Write short answers for these questions.

2. Where do algae usually grow? _____

3. What do fungi feed on? _____

4. Where would you find kelp? _____

5. Draw a line to match these sentence beginnings with their right endings.

Fungi often appear   is caused by algae growth.

You might find   algae and fungi in your backyard.

The green surface of a fishpond   after it has been raining.

6. Name three types of fungi.

a) _____   b) _____   c) _____

Name: _____   Date: _____

CLOZE EXERCISES

In cloze exercises, you have to select the best word to fill in the blank. To do cloze exercises well, you should read the title of the passage and the whole passage, as well as look at any pictures. When you have completed the exercise, read it again, from the beginning, to make sure it makes sense.

Read these passages and answer the questions. Circle the letter of the best answer.

Read this passage from *The Story of Camels in Australia* by Karen Lavelle.

> Because camels can drink large amounts of water when they do drink, people once thought they must be able to store ____(1)____ in their humps. "Not so," say scientists. "They just ____(2)____ what they have lost."
>
> When the temperature soars, the nose acts like a very effective heat exchange unit. It works to ____(3)____ the blood going to the camel's brain.

1. (A) food
   (B) water
   (C) energy
   (D) strength

2. (A) replace
   (B) control
   (C) store
   (D) reuse

3. (A) stop
   (B) smell
   (C) cool
   (D) boil

Read this passage from *Kites* by David Bowden and Jenny Dibley.

> People have always envied birds for their ability to fly.
>
> In 1893, human ____(4)____ finally became a possibility when Lawrence Hargrave invented the box kite. Fascinated by the idea of flying, he designed and ____(5)____ a succession of kites above the cliffs of Stanwell Park, south of Sydney.
>
> In 1894, he used four box kites to lift him five meters above the beach. The box kite, Hargrave's most famous ____(6)____, was the forerunner of the first successful airplane.

4. (A) flight
   (B) invention
   (C) law
   (D) work

5. (A) drew
   (B) sold
   (C) tested
   (D) piloted

6. (A) discovery
   (B) saying
   (C) report
   (D) invention

Read this passage from *The Tooth Book* by Viki Wright.

> The most famous false teeth in the world belonged to George Washington, who was born in 1732 and ____(7)____ in 1799. He became the first President of the United States in 1789. His problem with his ____(8)____ started around the time when the First Fleet was on its way to Australia and continued to worry him for the rest of his life. During a painful five-year period, he ____(9)____ all but one of his teeth.

7. (A) died   (B) lived
   (C) helped   (D) ruled

8. (A) birth   (B) world
   (C) teeth   (D) childhood

9. (A) found   (B) lost
   (C) cleaned   (D) used

Name: _____   Date: _____

SHINER
by Marilyn Cosgrove

You may have already read the following story, in which you practiced finding facts, using context clues, and drawing conclusions. Now read *Shiner* to try understanding questions. Then circle the letter to choose the best answer for each multiple-choice question.

Penny, the veterinarian, didn't recognize Shiner. She couldn't believe that any dog could survive for 25 days, trapped in a dark black hole without food.

Penny emerged from her surgery carrying a silent bundle. "She should sleep for hours and she will wake up feeling much better. Give her plenty of warm milk and keep her warm. She's a remarkable dog, but she couldn't have lasted much longer. I'd say she was unconscious for most of the time. She was lucky there was rainwater to drink. It saved her life—that and the fact that bull terriers are such a tough breed."

Back home, Shiner lay in a warm **nest** of blankets while Pat and George stared at her for hours. They were afraid to go to sleep in case they woke up to find it had all been a dream.

The local newspaper ran a story about "Shiner, the Wonder Dog." The neighborhood children brought her presents and placed them next to the weary Shiner. It was a week before her smile returned.

1. The veterinarian couldn't believe that Shiner

(A) belonged to Pat and George.

(B) lived for days trapped in a dark hole.

(C) could keep smiling for a week.

(D) would be in the newspaper.

2. Pat and George didn't sleep because

(A) they were waiting for the newspaper.

(B) they couldn't believe Shiner was really alive.

(C) children kept coming with presents.

(D) the vet told them that Shiner might die.

3. The vet gave Shiner something to make her

(A) eat.

(B) warm.

(C) smile.

(D) sleep.

4. In this story, the word "nest" means a place

(A) where birds sit on eggs.

(B) used by animals for sleeping.

(C) that is warm and safe.

(D) where animals spend the night.

5. How would you describe Pat and George? _____

Name: _____   Date: _____

INTRODUCTION

You might have already read the following story, in which you practiced finding the main idea, sequencing events, and drawing conclusions. Now let's read *Quiet Pony for Sale* to try **understanding paragraphs**.

We had an early look at paragraphs in Finding the Main Idea. Read page 14 again. Paragraphs indicate the introduction of new circumstances or people in the writing. New paragraphs usually show the introduction of:
  – a change of ideas or characters   – a change of place/setting   – a change of time
  – a change of action (what's happening)   – a change of speakers in conversation

Each new paragraph starts on a new line. In some writing, each new paragraph is indented. This means they start about 1 cm from the left margin. Paragraphs usually contain:
  – a topic sentence (See *Finding the Main Idea.*)
  – other sentences providing supporting details
  – two to ten sentences

Single sentence paragraphs are used for effect or in conversations.

Now read the story from *Quiet Pony for Sale* by Mary Small.

When Hannah came with her parents to live in the small country town of Bakers Flat, she had to catch the bus to school each day. On the first morning, while she was waiting at the end of the road for the bus to arrive, she saw a sign nailed to a gate on the other side of the highway. "Quiet pony for sale," it read. *(introduction of the main character)*

Hannah loved horses. That afternoon, back from school, she went to the gate and looked over. There in the middle of the paddock was the pony. His rough coat was matted with mud, his mane and tail were long and scraggly. He stared at her with sad brown eyes. *(introduction of another character — a pony)*

"Here, pony!" said Hannah, stretching out her hand. She felt annoyed that she had nothing to give him. *(conversations paragraph + new idea)*

The pony stood still. *(impact paragraph)*

"I'll bring you something tomorrow," said Hannah, and she hurried home. *(conversation paragraph)*

The next morning, she took two apples for her lunchbox. Back from school, she went straight to the gate. The pony was busy grazing. *(change of time)*

1. Write the number of sentences in each paragraph.

a) Paragraph 1: _____   b) Paragraph 2: _____   c) Paragraph 3: _____

d) Paragraph 4: _____   e) Paragraph 5: _____   f) Paragraph 6: _____

2. What words in paragraph 6 tell the reader there is a change in time? _____

3. Why do you think paragraph 4 is just one sentence? _____

_____

Answers:
1. a) 3 b) 5 c) 2 d) 1 e) 1 f) 3 2. The next morning 3. It is an important event in the story. It is the beginning of Hannah's association with the pony.

Name: _____   Date: _____

ALBERT'S BIRTHDAY
by Joan Dalgleish

You might have already read part of the following story, in which you practiced using context clues, drawing conclusions, and noting details. Now read *Albert's Birthday* to try understanding paragraphs.

After lunch on Thursday, Albert began to get ready. He pressed his brown pants, ironed his shirt, and shined his shoes. He searched through his chest of drawers for his best sweater. It smelled of mothballs, but a walk in the open air would soon fix that.

As he dressed, Albert began to feel very excited. It was just like the time all those years ago, when his aunt was coming to take him to the Christmas play.

In the fourth grade class, everyone was just as excited as Albert. All the tables had been moved to the middle of the room to form one long birthday table. The tablecloth was made by the children from pictures they had drawn, all taped together. The table was covered with plates of sweet bread, chocolate treats, individual cartons of juice, little iced cakes, sponge cakes, cinnamon rolls, and, of course, the birthday cake.

At five minutes to two, Miss Jones clapped her hands. "Quiet everyone! Over here to me, please."

The hubbub gradually died away.

When all the children were quiet, Miss Jones asked them all to thank all the people at home for helping to make the party food. Miss Jones herself had made a cake, with as many candles as she could fit around the words "Happy Birthday."

1. Write the number of sentences in each paragraph.

   a) Paragraph 1: _____   b) Paragraph 2: _____

   c) Paragraph 3: _____   d) Paragraph 4: _____

2. Write what each paragraph introduces. The first one is done for you.

   a) Paragraph 1: ___what's happening___   b) Paragraph 2: _____

   c) Paragraph 3: _____   d) Paragraph 4: _____

3. Paragraph 5 is used to

   ☐ show who is speaking.   ☐ introduce a new character.

   ☐ show a change in time.   ☐ highlight the importance of what is about to happen.

4. Paragraph 6 is mostly about

   ☐ the food the children ate.   ☐ the children being quiet.

   ☐ the people who supplied the food.   ☐ putting candles on a cake.

5. What is the topic sentence of paragraph 3? _____

_____

Name: _____   Date: _____

SPOOKED!
by Errol Broome

You might have already read the following story, in which you practiced finding the main idea. Now read *Spooked!* to try understanding paragraphs.

Gerry's house was the creepiest house on the street. It had rickety stairs and odd shaped rooms, full of dark corners, and a gabled roof that looked like a witch's hat. It was exactly the sort of place where you would expect to find something peculiar.

"I'm not scared," said Hank, who lived at number 37 Oak Street. He swung open Gerry's closet door. The hinges creaked, but the inside looked like any closet. It was a mess.

"There's nothing there," said Hank. "Just clothes and shoes and stuff."

Gerry didn't like the noises himself—not one bit. That's why he kept asking friends to stay. He had tried almost every boy on Oak Street, and they only came once. Now it was Hank's turn.

"Can't we leave the light on?" asked Hank. "That way we're sure to be safe."

"I've got a flashlight," said Gerry. "But okay, we can try the light too."

Rainy nights were the worst. The world outside was black, the trees switched like footsteps on the roof. The wind hissed. Rain clawed at the windows. It was creepy enough in the attic without the ghost in the closet too . . .

---

1. Write the number of sentences in the last paragraph. _____

2. The last paragraph introduces

☐ a character.   ☐ a place.

☐ a change in time.   ☐ someone speaking.

3. How are paragraphs 5 and 6 similar?

_____

4. Paragraph 4 is a new paragraph because it

☐ tells what is happening.   ☐ describes the house.

☐ records past events.   ☐ reports what the boys said.

5. Rewrite the shortest paragraph. _____

_____

6. Paragraph 2 is used to tell the reader about

☐ the house.   ☐ the weather.   ☐ messy cupboards.   ☐ Hank's behavior.

7. A paragraph with speech in it can have more than one sentence.   True ☐   False ☐

56

Name: _____   Date: _____

THE TOOTH BOOK
by Viki Wright

You might have already read part of the following passage, in which you practiced finding the main idea. Now read *The Tooth Book* to try understanding paragraphs.

How Much Is a Tooth Worth?

Teeth have always been regarded as valuable. Some ancient civilizations even had laws to compensate people whose teeth had been knocked out accidentally or in fights.

About 5,000 years ago the ancient Egyptians used to punish criminals by knocking out a front tooth. Honest people who knocked their front tooth out accidentally must have been very embarrassed by this because there are examples of mummies with carved wooden or ivory front teeth, tied in place with bits of silk thread. They would not have been able to bite with these, but at least they could smile like honest people.

About 4,000 years ago, in Ancient Babylon, there was a king called Hammurabi who invented the law of "an eye for an eye and a tooth for a tooth." This law put a value on various parts of a person's body. For example, if someone had a tooth knocked out in a fight, the person who had done the damage had to have one of his teeth knocked out in return.

About 3,000 years ago, in Asia Minor, the Hittites ruled that anyone who knocked out a citizen's tooth had to pay a fine of 20 pieces of silver. If he knocked out a slave's tooth, the fine was only 10 pieces of silver.

People have always known that teeth are valuable; in ancient times teeth were irreplaceable. For thousands of years, people have searched for ways to replace missing teeth with artificial ones.

1. This passage is about

☐ accidents involving loss of teeth.

☐ the ways modern people look after their teeth.

☐ the importance of teeth over the years.

☐ the punishments for committing a crime.

2. The second, third, and fourth paragraphs mainly introduce

☐ new characters.

☐ a change in action.

☐ a new topic.

☐ a new place and time.

3. Which paragraph describes the concern caused by missing teeth? paragraph _____

4. Which paragraph tells the reader the fine for knocking a slave's tooth out?

☐ paragraph 1   ☐ paragraph 2   ☐ paragraph 3   ☐ paragraph 4

5. The last paragraph describes (**replacing teeth**   **the value of teeth**). (Circle one answer.)

6. The setting for paragraph 2 is _____ and for paragraph 4 is _____ .

7. In your own words, tell how the first and last paragraphs are similar. _____

_____

Name: _____   Date: _____

INTRODUCTION

The following questions require an understanding of how the dictionary works and how to **use a dictionary**.

In dictionary-type exercises, you will have to find word meanings. You may use a dictionary or you may be expected to work out the meaning from the context of the story.

You will be expected to understand synonyms (similar meanings) and antonyms (opposites), make plurals, recognize words that have a number of meanings, know basic word building rules including affixes (prefixes/suffixes) and, of course, you must understand alphabetical order.

Now read the story from *Paddock for a Pony* by Elizabeth Best.

> They were very <u>uncomfortable</u>. It was only a small treehouse and three of them in at once made it extremely cramped.
>
> Mr. Crunkhorn was pacing now, up and down, up and down, still occasionally shouting that he would tell their parents and that he was going to wait until they came down and give them the whipping they deserved.
>
> Even so, in time they began to relax a little. At least he couldn't climb the tree after them.
>
> Billy whispered, "He's acting like a big property-owner with his hound-dogs — only he's just got two <u>silkies</u>."
>
> This made the girls giggle and the <u>tension</u> lifted further.

1. The word "tension" is closest in meaning to

☐ stress.   ☐ fear.   ☐ mood.   ☐ regret.

2. What does the prefix "un" mean in "uncomfortable"? _____

3. Write two more words that have the prefix "un."

a. _____   b. _____

4. The word "silkies" refers to the name of a type of

(A) material.   (B) dog.   (C) tree.

For questions 5 and 6, use the words below to answer the questions.

giggles   parents   further   shout   whipping

5. Circle the word that comes first in alphabetical order.

6. Draw a line under the word that would come last in alphabetical order.

7. The word "Crunkhorn" is not in the dictionary. Why not?

_____

Answers:

1. stress 2. not 3. Possible answers: unable, unused 4. (B) dog. 5. further 6. whipping 7. "Crunkhorn" would not be in the dictionary because it is a person's name.

Name: _____   Date: _____

QUIET PONY FOR SALE
by Mary Small

You might have already read part of the following story in which you practiced finding the main idea, sequencing events, drawing conclusions, and understanding paragraphs. Now read *Quiet Pony for Sale* to try using a dictionary.

When Hannah came with her parents to live in the small country town of Bakers Flat, she had to catch the bus to school each day. On the first morning, while she was waiting at the end of the road for the bus to arrive, she saw a **sign** nailed to a gate on the other side of the highway. "Quiet pony for sale," it read.

Hannah loved horses. That afternoon, back from school, she went to the gate and looked over. There in the middle of the paddock was the pony. His rough coat was **matted with mud**, his mane and tail were long and scraggly.

He stared at her with sad brown eyes.

"Here, pony!" said Hannah, stretching out her hand. She felt annoyed that she had nothing to give him.

The pony stood still.

"I'll bring you something tomorrow," said Hannah, and she hurried home.

Next morning, she took two apples for her lunchbox. Back from school, she went straight to the gate. The pony was busy **grazing**.

Sometimes, to get the alphabetical order of words right, you have to go to the second letter. The words "hat" and "hurt" both start with "h." If you look at the next letters, you will see they are "a" and "u"; "a" comes before "u" so "h<u>a</u>t" comes before "h<u>u</u>rt."

For questions 1 and 2, use the words to answer the questions.

    school   stared   she   sign   saw

1. Circle the word that comes first in alphabetical order.

2. Draw a line under the word that would come last in alphabetical order.

3. In the story, the word "grazing" is closest in meaning to

☐ eating.   ☐ trotting.   ☐ planting.   ☐ finding.

4. If something is "matted with mud," it

☐ is flat and dirty.   ☐ has mud all through it.   ☐ is warm and cuddly.

5. In the story, the word "sign" could be replaced with

☐ look.   ☐ watch.   ☐ poster.   ☐ listen.

6. Find a word in the story that means "to go somewhere without wasting time."

_____

Name: _____   Date: _____

ALBERT'S BIRTHDAY

by Joan Dalgleish

You might have already read part of the following story, in which you practiced using context clues, drawing conclusions, noting details, and understanding paragraphs. Now read *Albert's Birthday* to try using a dictionary.

With great excitement, Albert put on his glasses and began to open the envelopes. The cards all wished him happy birthday and sent good wishes for the future.

Albert stood the cards up all around the house—on the mantelpiece, the small tables, the bathroom shelf, the window ledges, and even on the kitchen sink.

By eleven o'clock Albert decided he needed a rest. He sat back in his armchair with a cup of tea and a cookie. He was very happy, but he was also very tired. Soon, he nodded off to sleep.

R-r-ring! R-r-ring! The doorbell woke him.

"Goodness me, surely not more cards? Wherever will I put them?"

Albert opened the door to find a young woman standing on his doorstep, and his front yard full of children.

"Hello, Albert," smiled the young woman. "Happy birthday!"

"Happy birthday, Albert!" **cried** all the children.

For questions 1 through 3, use the words below to answer the questions.

   soon   stood   sat   surely   smiled

1. Circle the word that comes first in alphabetical order.

2. Draw a line under the word that would come last in alphabetical order.

3. Put an X on the word that comes next after "smiled."

4. In the story, the word "cried" could best be replaced with

☐ wept.   ☐ shouted.   ☐ moaned.   ☐ said.

5. Compound words are made from two small words joined together. For example: bath +

   room = bathroom. Find two other examples. a. _____ b. _____

Circle the letter next to the word that best completes each sentence.

> At five minutes to two, Miss Jones clapped her hands. "Quiet everyone! Over here to me, please."
>
> When all the ___(6)___ were quiet, Miss Jones asked them to remember to ___(7)___ all the people at home for helping to make the ___(8)___ food. Miss Jones herself had made a cake with as many candles as she could fit on it.

6. (A) children
     (B) hands
     (C) clapping
     (D) clocks

7. (A) thank
     (B) take
     (C) help
     (D) find

8. (A) dog
     (B) frozen
     (C) party
     (D) fast

Name: _____   Date: _____

HO, HO, HO!

by Jan Weeks

You might have already read part of the following play, in which you practiced sequencing events. Now read *Ho, Ho, Ho!* to try using a dictionary.

Booming from somewhere up in the North Pole,
The voice said: "My pants have sprung a huge hole!
You could **park** a gigantic battleship there!
It's against the law — a crime, do you hear?
For a man like me to be exposed, dear!
How can I possibly go, 'Ho, ho, ho!'
With my underpants all out on show?"

Then Santa himself appeared at the door,
Hands covering the rip, which tore a bit more.
With forehead so wrinkled and face so cross,
He sputtered, "Is this how you treat your boss?
One of you elves must be playing a joke—
A mighty **mean** thing to do to a bloke!
This can't be the same suit I wore last year,
When spreading around all that Christmas cheer."

"You only have to use your eyes
To see this suit's not the proper size."

1. Circle the word that would come before "cheer" in alphabetical order.

gigantic   bloke   crime   spluttered   joke

2. Circle the first word that would come after "hole" in alphabetical order.

law   is   huge   rear   elves

3. Find three compound words in the poem.   a. _____

b. _____   c. _____

4. The word "park," as used in the poem, means

☐ an open area with grass and trees.   ☐ ground where sports are played.

☐ to leave until required.   ☐ a place designed for cars.

5. Circle the answer that best completes the sentence.

Santa thought the elves were (up to mischief   being lazy   not doing their job properly).

6. In the poem, the word "mean" could be replaced with

☐ explain.   ☐ nasty.   ☐ stingy.   ☐ unfair.

Name: _____   Date: _____

INTRODUCTION

Most factual books have a **table of contents**. It is found in the front of the book, usually within the first few pages. A table of contents is a quick reference that helps readers find the main sections of the book. Some books are broken up into major sections or subjects or topics and, within each section or subject area, there are subsections.

Some fiction books may also have a table of contents. These may give the location of the chapters or, if a book has many works, the place in the book of the individual stories, plays, or poems.

Here is a table of contents from *Dugong, Dive* by Jill Morris.

major subject headings

A **glossary** is found at the back of a book. It lists, alphabetically, and explains unusual words found in the book.

Table of Contents

page numbers

what is found in each section

Some books also have an **index** which is an alphabetical list of subtopics and references to be found in the book. The index will include page numbers.

1. On what page would you find "Dugong Song"? _____

2. Under what heading would you find facts about dugongs? _____

3. The section, Prose Poem, begins on page 2.   True ☐ False ☐

4. The Mermaid Connection is in the chapter called "Pourquoi Tale." True ☐ False ☐

5. What page would you turn to start reading the story "Why the Dugong Lives in the Sea"?

_____

Answers:
1. page 16 2. Report 3. True 4. False 5. page 18

Understanding and using a table of contents

Name: _____   Date: _____

FUN WITH FOOD
by Eleanor Parker

Table of Contents

1. On what page will you find the index? _____

2. On what page will you find out how to make Fruit Cream Cheese? _____

3. What is the last recipe in the book? _____

4. The word "sprouts" is used in the book. Where would I first look to find all references to sprouts in the book? _____ .

5. How many "Fun Foods to Make for Special Occasions" are listed? _____

6. What is the section called that starts on page 22? _____

7. Where in the book would you find the table of contents? _____ .

Name: _____   Date: _____

INTRODUCTION

Schedules play an important part in our lives. We have schedules for each day at school. We have schedules for sports days and swim meets. The program for the school concert is a schedule.

Some of us use schedules for bus or train travel. Without schedules we could be late for school or work. We could miss out on things we want to do. Schedules help us to keep our lives in order.

This schedule shows what Jenny's class does on a Friday. Read it and answer the questions.

Learning Points

A.M. is in the morning

P.M. is in the afternoon

From a schedule, you can find out how long things take. For example, music takes 30 minutes (half an hour).

Time	Subject
9:30 A.M.	Free Choice Silent Reading
9:45 A.M.	Math Groups
10:15 A.M.	Music (Ms. French), Room M
10:45 A.M.	Spelling Test
11:00 A.M.	**RECESS**
11:20 A.M.	English
12:20 P.M.	Individual Projects
12:45 P.M.	**LUNCH**
1:30 P.M.	Weekly Assembly
2:00 P.M.	Sports (softball/volleyball teams)
3:15 P.M.	Announcements/Notes
3:25 P.M.	End of Lessons
3:35 P.M.	After-School Sports Coaching

Give short answers for questions 1 through 6.

1. What time does Jenny start school? _____   **2.** How long is recess? _____ minutes

3. What does the class have after recess? _____

4. Which activity is the longest? _____

5. What teacher teaches the class for music? _____

6. When does math end? _____

7. If Jenny has to wait at school after 3:30 P.M., she could go to _____ .

8. On Friday, Jenny has a _____ test at _____ .

Answers:

1. 9:30 A.M. 2. 20 3. English 4. sports 5. Ms. French 6. 10:15 A.M. 7. sports coaching 8. spelling; 10:45 A.M.

Name: _____   Date: _____

TRAIN SCHEDULE

To ride a bus or and train, you might need to read a schedule.

CRYSTAL CITY to GRAND CENTRAL
Schedule for Mondays, Wednesdays, and Fridays

TRAIN FROM		A.M.	A.M.	P.M.	P.M.	P.M.
Crystal City	♿	6:30	9:30	12:30	3:30	6:30
Loren		6:40	9:40		3:40	6:40
Lukes Crossing	♿	7:10	10:10	1:00	4:10	7:10
Bindi Fields		7:25	10:25		4:25	7:25
Holly Glen	♿	7:40	10:40	1:30	4:40	7:40
Alantown		7:55	10:55		4:55	7:55
Grand Central	♿	8:05	11:05	1:50	5:05	8:05

Give short answers for questions 1 through 8.

1. How many morning trips are there from Crystal City to Grand Central? _____

2. At what time does the 9:30 A.M. train arrive at Grand Central? _____

3. At what time does the 9:30 A.M. train arrive at Holly Glen? _____

4. On how many days each week do trains run from Crystal City to Grand Central? _____

5. What is the last train you can catch if you have to get to Grand Central by 3:30 P.M.? _____

6. How long does the 3:30 P.M. train take to get from Loren to Bindi Fields? _____ minutes

7. The train that leaves Holly Glen at 7:40 P.M. gets to Alantown at _____ .

8. The longest part of the journey is between _____ and _____ .

9. The last train on Friday does not stop at Lukes Crossing.   True ☐   False ☐

10. The 12:30 P.M. train stops at Bindi Fields.   True ☐   False ☐

11. Explain what this sign (♿) means. _____

_____

12. How long does the 9:30 A.M. train take to go from Crystal City to Grand Central?

_____

13. Why do you think the 12:30 P.M. train is quicker than the other trains? _____

_____

Page 6: Finding Facts—Introduction
1. A dugong is an aquatic mammal.
2. Dugongs live in water (or the sea).
3. size
4. flippers
5. The tusks (of the male) are used for defense.

Page 7: Finding Facts—Hearty Facts
1. The passage is about the human heart.
2. A normal heart beats 60 to 80 times a minute.
3. A child's heart beats 100 to 120 times each minute.
4. The heart pumps blood to every part of the body.
5. Answers will vary.

Page 8: Finding Facts—Kites
1. Kites were first used in China.
2. Kites were used in war for military purposes.
3. False
4. True
5. True
6. military, monsters, measuring

Page 9: Finding Facts—Golden Wombats
1. She was trying to solve the mystery of the golden wombats.
2. Most of the wombats are silver-grey.
3. Possible answers: has changed with age/been bleached by the sun/is a result of diet
4. Jill Morris saw her first golden wombat in a field on the east coast of Flinders Island.
5. She also saw them on a hillside.

Page 10: Finding Facts—Bobby Boy
1. Tommy Woodcock worked in the stables.
2. (C) Tommy Woodcock's character.
3. Mr. Telford was the owner of Phar Lap and the stables.
4. It means lightning.
5. He treated the horses kindly or with care.
6. win the Melbourne Cup.

Page 11: Finding Facts—Shiner
1. be a pup that lived outdoors.
2. looked as if she had a black eye.
3. George got his black eye in a wrestling match.
4. False
5. True

Page 12: Finding Facts—Names Are Fun
1. Many people forget other people's names.
2. Ben-Chris-Kim
3. The writer of the extract. OR The sister of Stan and Howard.
4. Parents have so much to think about — they haven't done it on purpose.
   Some people who forget names — they can forget their children's names.
   If friends forget your name, — have bad memories.
5. stumble
6. forgotten
7. worry (or bother)
8. False

Page 13: Finding Facts—A Monster Will Get You

1. The Kongkoi is a monster that lives in the forest in Laos.
2. The gwee live in ponds and rivers in China and Thailand.
3. people in Australia come from many different cultures.
4. True
5. True
6. have been passed down through the ages.

Page 14: Finding the Main Idea—Introduction

1. four
2. four
3. a. poor   b. straggly (Other possible answers: lame/limping, yearling)
4. The New Horse

Page 15: Finding the Main Idea—Quiet Pony for Sale

1. seven
2. Hannah loved horses.
3. went with an apple to see the pony.
4. how Hannah came to see the notice.
5. The pony looked at her with sad eyes.
6. Making Friends
7. Suggested answer: It's the first meeting of the two characters.

Page 16: Finding the Main Idea—Bobby Boy

1. five
2. Paragraph 1 — Phar Lap comes to the USA.
   Paragraph 2 — Phar Lap becomes a hero.
   Paragraph 3 — Phar Lap dies.
   Paragraph 4 — Phar Lap gets sick.
3. The Death of Phar Lap
4. Paragraph 2
5. (A) The news flashed to Australia: *Phar Lap is dead!*

Page 17: Finding the Main Idea—Cunning Running

1. eight
2. Orienteering began in Australia in 1969.
3. Let's Learn About Orienteering
4. What Is Orienteering?
5. True

Page 18: Finding the Main Idea—Joanne

1. It is about Joanne's father and mother.
2. Joanne's life with her father
3. sharing.
4. Joanne.
5. True
6. False

Page 19: Finding the Main Idea—The Tooth Book

1. six
2. Different people tried to do parts of the work that dentists do today.
3. first — the Phoenicians
   second — the Egyptians
   third — the Etruscans
4. five
5. The History of False Teeth

Page 20: Finding the Main Idea—Spooked!

1. six
2. Main Idea — rickety stairs
   — a gabled roof that looked like a witch's hat
   Supporting Details — description of Gerry's house
   — dark corners
3. Gerry's reason for inviting friends to sleep over.
4. two
5. Brave Hank
6. False

Page 21: Finding the Main Idea—Mr. Greyfinch's Garden

1. Paragraph 1 — the garden
   Paragraph 3 — moving in
   Paragraph 5 — the new home
2. paragraph 3 or paragraph 4
3. Moving to a New House
4. False
5. False
6. unpacked his belongings

Page 22: Sequencing—Introduction

1. Hannah saw a sign nailed to a gate on the other side of the highway.
2. Hannah put two apples in her lunchbox.
3. stood still
4. A. Hannah and her parents went to live in the country.

Page 23: Sequencing—Charlie's Fish and Other Tales

1. Charlie headed for the river bend as soon as he had unloaded the cart.
2. 4 Charlie tried to land the giant fish.
   3 Charlie tied his fishing line to the horse team.
   2 Charlie woke up by the sound of waves crashing.
   1 Charlie waited for three days.
3. Charlie unpacked his cart.
4. False
5. True
6. (B) early hours of the morning
7. 5

Page 24: Sequencing—Numbering Exercises

1. *The Day My Friend Learned to Dance* by Hazel Edwards
   2 I nodded, and he followed me.
   1 Jason looked uncomfortable. "Is it okay if we go in?" he whispered.
   3 Mom and Dad were behind us.
2. *Your Backyard Jungle* by Kerrie Bingle, David Bowden, and Jenny Dibley
   2 In some species, the female keeps the eggs in her body and produces live young.
   3 Young insects grow and develop in three different ways.
   1 All insects begin life as an egg.
3. *Mitsina, the Hermit* by David Shapiro
   1 Long ago, before men and women lived on Earth, gods and goddesses lived in heaven.
   3 Sharp-sighted Mitsina was an evil god.
   2 But not all gods and goddesses were good.
4. *Spooked!* by Errol Broome
   2 The boys' scalps prickled.
   1 The doors rattled again.
   3 They held their breath, waiting for something to happen.
   4 Surely something had moved inside the closet.

5. *Quiet Pony for Sale* by Mary Small
   3 When he was alone in the garden, he was afraid that Mrs. Jenkin's cat would creep up and then jump in his lap.
   1 Derek was afraid of animals.
   2 He was born unable to walk, so spent most of his time in a wheelchair.
   4 The first time it had happened he had screamed in terror at the cat.

Page 25: Sequencing—Boat Boy
1. First ——————— The children screamed when Lisa's lizard escaped.
   Second ————— Mrs. Bramble reminded the class to bring their grandparents.
   Third ————— The class drew invitations.
   Fourth ————— Dieu threw his invitation away.
2. The next special day was going to be Grandparents' Day.
3. 1 Mrs. Bramble said, "Tomorrow is another of our special days."
   3 Mrs. Bramble said, "Remember those invitations you drew last week?"
   2 Mrs. Bramble said, "Tomorrow is Grandparents' Day."
4. False

Page 26: Sequencing—A Night at Benny's
1. She made a fuss about Brian going to Benny's place.
2. First ————— Dad was hit with a stream of soapsuds.
   Second ————— The narrator packs his overnight bag.
   Third ————— The narrator and Benny slammed the door.
   Fourth ————— Fiona was told not to complain.
3. Fiona complained loudly.
4. Fiona hit her father with soapsuds.
5. False
6. False
7. night

Page 27: Sequencing—Ho, Ho, Ho!
1. cold
2. week
3. pants
4. not
5. 1 The weather had turned very cold.
   3 The silence was broken by a booming voice.
   2 Santa discovered a hole.
6. winter
7. True
8. False
9. False

Page 28: Using Context Clues—Introduction
1. a) hot water bottles b) ticking clocks
2. enjoyable
3. soft-hearted.
4. confused

Page 29: Using Context Clues—Pets' Day
1. care
2. thinking.
3. she was getting teaching experience.
4. noisy/rude/naughty
5. on top of the cupboard

Page 30: Using Context Clues—Albert's Birthday
1. a) he shuffled slowly b) he wheezed or his bones creaked
2. The message pad was blank.
3. in the morning
4. having trouble breathing
5. in the city.
6. False
7. True

Page 31: Using Context Clues—Dragons of China
1. exist nowhere but in people's minds.
2. hatched from an egg that laid on the land for a thousand years.
3. spiritual dragon
4. True
5. False
6. human

Page 32: Using Context Clues—Jack Finds the Outback
1. a) not many people b) huge space that's mainly sand
2. inquisitive.
3. False
4. True
5. False
6. True

Page 33: Using Context Clues—The Day My Friend Learned to Dance
1. Suggested answer: about 8
2. His class plays T-ball, which is often played before learning softball.
3. eat it
4. people did what they were told.
5. Possible answer: The Invitation
6. school.
7. uneasy
8. False
9. False

Page 34: Drawing Conclusions—Introduction
1. Possible answers: He is content that he has had a long life, or he accepts his limitations, or has a pet dog that he cares for
2. He didn't go looking for her; he found things to laugh about
3. contented
4. Old Friends

Page 35: Drawing Conclusions—Charlie's Fish and Other Tales
1. (C) The explosion knocked the miners' fillings out of their mouths.
   (D) The miners recognized their gold fillings.
2. His eyes nearly popped out of his head.
3. comedian; Bill is trying to make people laugh.
4. The explosion knocked the miners' fillings out. Bill found the fillings in the stream. The fillings were quite large.

Page 36: Drawing Conclusions—Joanne
1. (D) excitement in his voice
2. Dad started work at 5 A.M.; He worked until 2:30 P.M.
3. was; Most nights Dad telephoned.
4. dedicated, determined

Page 37: Drawing Conclusions—Quiet Pony for Sale

1. (A) excited, (C) giggled
2. Derek clung to his mother.
3. (A) The ponies were all very quiet.
   (B) The children were greeted when they arrived.
   (C) The riding school had the ponies ready.
   (E) Mrs. Harvey encouraged the children to join in.
4. Derek was frightened of the horses. (shy)
5. kind
6. well-prepared

Page 38: Drawing Conclusions—Bobby Boy

1. (A) He won eight races in nine weeks.
   (D) He carried more weight than any other horse in the race.
2. Possible answers: distressed, upset, or worried
3. with
4. Phar Lap carried 68 kilograms in the race. Phar Lap had won a race two days earlier.
5. He was off to conquer the world.

Page 39: Drawing Conclusions—Shiner

1. (D) The neighbor was understanding about the loss of the dog.
   (E) The neighbor didn't protest about the work George was doing.
2. The neighbor — wanted a flashlight to look under the house.
   George — was first to realize where the dog might be.
   Pat — put out a saucer of milk for the stray cat.
3. Pat: let out a shriek
4. George: wanted a flashlight in a hurry
5. False

Page 40: Noting Details—Introduction

1. The details that tell the reader that Albert cares are: the flap in the door so Missy can come and go whenever she likes; Albert's search around the yard for Missy; Albert knows Missy's habits well (where she lies to enjoy the sun).
2. Possible answer: The house is surrounded by tall buildings.
3. Albert has just had tea and toast for breakfast; the sun was not high in the sky; Missy may have left the house before Albert got up to get some morning sun.
4. He took a lot of care in getting his clothes ready.
5. Albert had to search for his sweater. It was probably in the bottom of the drawer. It had been in moth balls. Some people do this to keep moths away from their clothes if they aren't going to wear them for a long time.

Page 41: Noting Details—The Story of Camels in Australia

1. horses — sport
   pigs — transport
   foxes — pets
   cats — food
2. They were brought here by people.
3. domesticated
4. as stowaways
5. Possible answers: pigs, cattle, sheep, rats, mice, horses
6. People brought animals and <u>plants</u> to Australia for a number of reasons. They brought pigs and <u>cattle/sheep</u> to provide food. Horses could be used for hunting, but they were also used to <u>transport</u>. Rats came to Australia as stowaways on the <u>ships</u> that also brought people.

Page 42: Noting Details—Dinky-Di

1. strange land — lively expressions
   hard life — humorous expressions
   modern Australians — new expressions

2. used slang from their homelands to communicate.
3. False
4. True
5. True
6. True
7. False

Page 43: Noting Details—TV News

1. editors — main news
   promo — news advertisement
   scripts — select the film for the news
2. False
3. False
4. False
5. False
6. True
7. a) scripts b) promos
8. above

Page 44: Noting Details—A Night at Benny's

1. Felicity — throws soapsuds at Brian (the narrator)
   Benny — nickname is Creep Features
   Fiona — tells Fiona to wash and dry the dishes
   Dad — uses the bed as a trampoline
2. 3 teased Fiona, 1 got invited to Benny's place, 2 packed his bag
3. False
4. False
5. enemies
6. smug
7. Brian is mischievous because he intentionally irritates his sister.
8. It took about half an hour to get to Benny's place.

Page 45: Noting Details—In the Made-Up World

1. Maurice Mouse
2. cattery
3. purr
4. scares cats
5. a. wash his cars b. bring him cheese c. patrol his house/wait on him/call him "Sir"
6. False
7. False
8. he finds he has been dreaming.
9. (D) cats.

Page 46: Following Directions—Introduction

1. five steps
2. eight
3. These directions help you make Peta Pea Soup.
4. alfalfa sprouts

Page 47: Following Directions—Banana Delight Ice Cream

1. seven
2. two
3. six
4. Suggested answer: These instructions show how to make Banana Delight Ice Cream.
5. ingredients
6. put
7. put the mixture in a covered container.

8. lemon juice.
9. True
10. True

Page 48: Following Directions—How to Be a Magician
1. four
2. three
3. fishing line
4. perform, talk
5. magic
6. False
7. 2 Cover a table with a cloth.
   1 Collect the props.
   4 Place the bangle bracelet under the tablecloth.
   3 Tie a long thread to a bangle bracelet.

Page 49: Following Directions—Growing Your Own Sprouts
1. Put the seeds in the jar. Cover the top of the jar with a cloth and secure it tightly with a rubber band.
2. sprout seeds
3. The final step is to give the sprouts a final rinse.
4. 2 Put the seeds in the jar in a dark place.
   4 Keep the seeds moist as they germinate.
   3 Bring the seeds into the sunlight.
   1 Soak the seeds in warm water.
5. hold the cloth cover in place
6. True

Page 50: Understanding Questions—Introduction
1. The accident happened at a pedestrian crossing in front of the general store.
2. Joanne's father ——————————— were lying on the road.
   Joanne was on her way home ——— was trying to comfort Jack.
   Scotty and Jack ———————— when she heard the siren.
3. False
4. holding, licking

Page 51: Understanding Questions—Your Backyard Jungle: Plants
1. **Algae**   **Fungi**
   kelp   mushrooms
   seaweed   toadstools
   fishpond   dead leaves
   salt water   yeast
   contains chlorophyll mold
2. in water
3. dead or dying plant matter
4. in the ocean
5. Fungi often appear ——————— is caused by algae growth.
   You might find ——————— algae and fungi in your backyard.
   The green surface of a fishpond ——— after it has been raining.
6. molds, toadstools, mushrooms or yeast

Page 52: Understanding Questions—Cloze Exercises
1. (B) water
2. (A) replace
3. (C) cool
4. (A) flight
5. (C) tested
6. (D) invention

7. (A) died

8. (C) teeth

9. (B) lost

Page 53: Understanding Questions—Shiner

1. (B) lived for days trapped in a dark hole.
2. (B) they couldn't believe Shiner was really alive.
3. (D) sleep.
4. (C) that is warm and safe.
5. Suggested answer: Pat and George are very grateful people.

Page 54: Understanding Paragraphs—Introduction

1. a) 3   b) 5   c) 2   d) 1   e) 1   f) 3
2. The next morning
3. It is an important event in the story. It is the beginning of Hannah's association with the pony.

Page 55: Understanding Paragraphs—Albert's Birthday

1. a) 4   b) 2   c) 4   d) 3
2. a) Paragraph 1: what's happening   b) Paragraph 2: change in time and action
   c) Paragraph 3: new characters   d) Paragraph 4: Miss Jones speaks
3. highlight the importance of what is about to happen.
4. the people who supplied the food.
5. In the fourth grade class, everyone was just as excited as Albert.

Page 56: Understanding Paragraphs—Spooked!

1. five
2. a change in time.
3. Each paragraph has someone speaking.
4. tells what is happening.
5. "I've got a flashlight," said Gerry. "But okay, we can try the light too."
6. Hank's behavior.
7. True

Page 57: Understanding Paragraphs—The Tooth Book

1. the importance of teeth over the years.
2. a new place and time.
3. two
4. paragraph 4
5. the value of teeth
6. Egypt, Asia Minor
7. They are similar because they both emphasize the value of teeth over time.

Page 58: Using a Dictionary—Introduction

1. stress.
2. not
3. Possible answers: unable, unused
4. (B) dog.
5. further
6. whipping
7. "Crunkhorn" would not be in the dictionary because it is a person's name.

Page 59: Using a Dictionary—Quiet Pony for Sale

1. saw
2. stared
3. eating.
4. has mud all through it.
5. poster.
6. straight

Page 60: Using a Dictionary—Albert's Birthday
1. sat
2. surely
3. soon
4. shouted.
5. Possible answers: armchair, birthday, doorstep, mantelpiece, doorbell
6. (A) children
7. (A) thank
8. (C) party

Page 61: Using a Dictionary—Ho, Ho, Ho!
1. bloke
2. huge
3. battleship, himself, underpants, forehead, or somewhere
4. to leave until required.
5. up to mischief
6. nasty.

Page 62: Understanding and Using a Table of Contents—Introduction
1. page 16
2. Report
3. True
4. False
5. page 18

Page 63: Understanding and Using a Table of Contents—Fun with Food
1. page 34
2. page 23
3. Moon Craters
4. in the index
5. eight
6. Making Your Own Cheese
7. in the front

Page 64: Using Schedules—Introduction
1. 9:30 A.M.
2. 20
3. English
4. sports
5. Ms. French
6. 10:15 A.M.
7. sports coaching
8. spelling, 10:45 A.M.

Page 65: Using Schedules—Train Schedule
1. two
2. 11:05 A.M.
3. 10:40 A.M.
4. three
5. 12:30 P.M.
6. 45
7. 7:55 P.M.
8. Loren, Lukes Crossing
9. False
10. False
11. People in wheelchairs have easy access to the station and train.
12. 1 hour 35 minutes (95 minutes)
13. The 12:30 train only stops at three stations.

Name: _____   Date: _____

5 Ws AND 1 H

Use this organizer to help you **find facts** so you can visualize information, thoughts, and ideas. Read an article or passage and use this organizer to answer the questions *who, what, why, where, when,* and *how*.

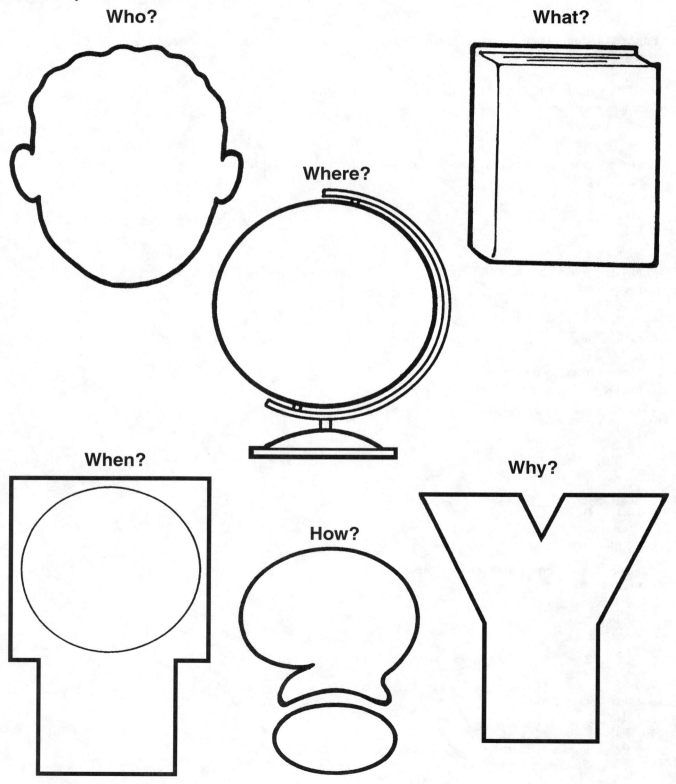

Who?

What?

Where?

When?

Why?

How?

Name: _____   Date: _____

ON TARGET

Read your article or passage. **Find the main idea** and write it in the center. Then find the supporting details and write them around the main idea.

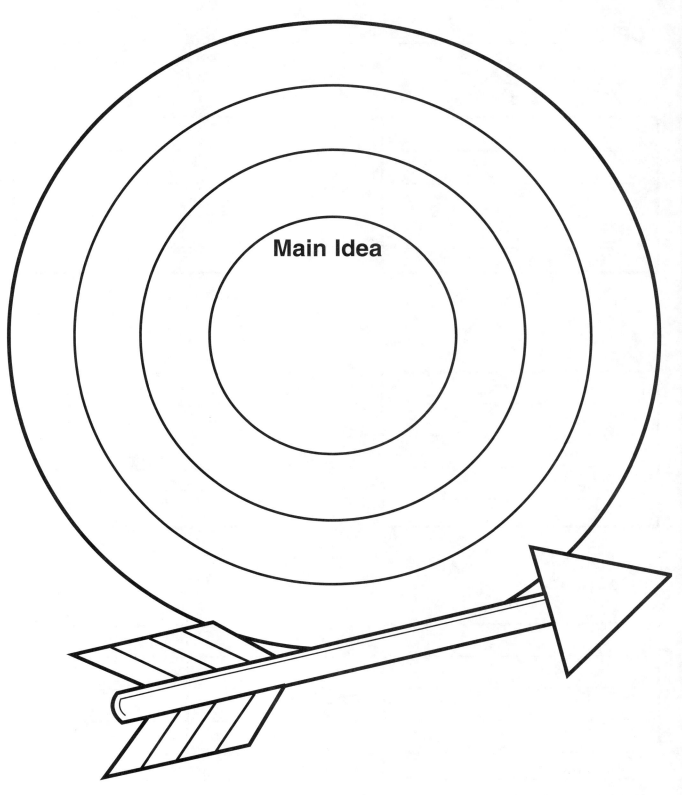

Main Idea

Name: _____   Date: _____

MAKING PROGRESS

Use this simple chart to help with **sequencing**. Choose your topic and list the steps/events in order. This will help organize your thoughts and teach you how to pay attention to words such as *first, second*, etc.

TOPIC: _____

1

2

3

4

5

6

Name: _____   Date: _____

PARAGRAPH ORGANIZER

Use this web to organize your thoughts and help you **understand paragraphs**. Write down the main topic of the article or passage. Then read each paragraph and find the supporting topic and all the details.

The Main Topic

_____

Supporting Topic

Details

Supporting Topic

Details

Supporting Topic

Details

Name: _____ Date: _____

I KNOW WHAT THAT MEANS!

Use this form to help you **use a dictionary**. Find a word that is new to you in your article or passage. Then write what you think it means on the "My Guess" line. Look up the word in the dictionary. If your guess was right, check the box. If not, write what the word means on the lines under the checkbox. Find another word and do the same.

Word: _____

My guess: _____

_____

_____

I guessed right! ❏

Now I know it means _____

_____

_____

Word: _____

My guess: _____

_____

_____

I guessed right! ❏

Now I know it means _____

_____

_____

Word: _____

My guess: _____

_____

_____

I guessed right! ❏

Now I know it means _____

_____

_____

Word: _____

My guess: _____

_____

_____

I guessed right! ❏

Now I know it means _____

_____

_____

GRAPHIC ORGANIZERS

#8044 Strategies That Work! 80 ©Teacher Created Resources, Inc.